CCCC
CCCC**CONVIVIUM**PRESS
CCCC

José Ignacio González Faus

Builders of Community: Rethinking Ecclesiastical Ministry

Translated by María Isabel Reyna
Revised by Liam Kelly

CONVIVIUMPRESS

SERIES TRADITIO

2012

Builders of Community:
Rethinking Ecclesiastical Ministry

© José Ignacio González Faus

http://www.conviviumpress.com
sales@conviviumpress.com
ventas@conviviumpress.com
convivium@conviviumpress.com

7661 NW 68th St, Suite 108,
Miami, Florida 33166. USA.
Phone: +1 (305) 8890489
Fax: +1 (305) 8875463

Edited by Rafael Luciani
Translated by María Isabel Reyna
Revised by Liam Kelly
Designed by Eduardo Chumaceiro d'E
Series: *Traditio*

ISBN: 978-1-934996-25-6

Printed in Colombia
Impreso en Colombia
D'VINNI, S.A.

Convivium Press
Miami, 2012

Builders of Community:
Rethinking Ecclesiastical
Ministry

Contents

3

The Clericalization of the Ministry *PAGE* 95

4

Conclusions for Today PAGE *141*

«*Precisely because within the Church's life the priest is a man of communion, in his relations with all people he must be a man of mission and dialogue…, the priest is called to witness in all his relationships to fraternity, service and a common quest for the truth, as well as a concern for the promotion of justice and peace*».

JOHN PAUL II

Pastores dabo vobis, 25 March 1992, n. 18

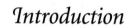 *Introduction*

1

The Hour of Crisis

Despite its length, or precisely because of it, this book has few aspirations to originality. It does not attempt, either in its exegetical or in its historical analysis, to affirm anything that is not already known or at least sufficiently accepted by scholars. It does, however, offer something new in two areas. First, in the attempt to *put together* and unify many of these positions accepted today (on various occasions others have also undertaken this with different emphases). Secondly, in the objective of this work of systematization: to *learn* from the history of the Church for our current missionary task.

So the gathering of information is not done to gain knowledge or academic perfection. Doubtless many facts are missing (some because of my own limited knowledge and others due to the forced selection imposed by the aspect of this work), but I do hope that those which appear here will be sufficient to justify the conclusions. I would like to underline that this brief look at the past endeavors to enlighten the present moment of the Church, marked —as far as our topic is concerned— by three significant sets of problems.

1.1. THE CURRENT CRISIS IN MINISTRY

I believe this crisis does exist and that it is a crisis of identity. I am not reassured by the argument that the crisis of ministry is a false problem, created by the Church in denying the ordination of married men, and that it would disappear if the Church ever took this step. Regardless of what could be said about this issue, I think that it is pointless to have a married clergy within the Church if we are not absolutely clear why they might be ordained. To reduce stereotypically this «why» to the celebration of the Eucharist will only deepen the sacramental-ist crisis experienced today by many ministers. It would also reduce the ecclesial ministry to a mere functionary role not very appealing either with or without celibacy.

In this sense, much of what is written in this book, though grounded in the New Testament and in Church history, is part also of what has been, more than once, my personal testimony —more friendly than academic— with many young theology students or candidates for priesthood when the time for the final decision, to be ordained or not, and why, came up.

I would also like to acknowledge that this book received a final stimulus from Ch. Duquoc's excellent article «*La reforma de los clérigos*» (in vvaa, *La recepción del Vaticano ii*, Cristianidad, Madrid 1987, 355-367). This article by Duquoc is one of the most clear and insightful descriptions of the current crisis in ministry and of how this crisis came about after Vatican ii. But the task set by Duquoc's analysis cannot be undertaken swiftly and at the first attempt, so to speak. A slow process of reconstruction, of recovery and also sometimes —in this sense— of demolition will be needed. I have already pointed out that many others have attempted this job. My reflections are presented here only as a first step in that direction to which surely one must return (this is expressed by the bias of the subtitle: «re-thinking ecclesial ministry»; of course many others can also be tempted).

The important point of this digression was to suggest to the reader that maybe it would be interesting to read Duquoc's article before (or also).

1.2.   THE CURRENT CRISIS AMONG THE LAITY

This is just the reverse of the previous one, which the 1987 Synod of Bishops presented again for discussion. In truth, the notion of «laity» correlates totally to the notion of «clergy» and the changes in the latter necessarily impact on the definition and identity of the former.

Furthermore, it is more than likely that the Church is reaching what has been called «the hour of the laity». But it is also possible that we might pass over this moment fruitlessly not aware that it happened or in what it consisted.

1.3.   THE CHURCH'S WAY OF BEING IN THE WORLD

In the end this work is motivated by a personal concern (which I think is very much shared) about *the mode of the Church's presence in the world*. «Christendom» destroyed without the possibility of going back, there is no finished model with which to substitute it. This has led many people to consider the restorationism of the aforementioned «Christendom», trying to be of service to the Church; but these efforts, in my opinion, can cause almost irreparable historical damage to the Church.

So, in this context I have come to the personal conclusion that there is an implicit parallelism in the form of relationship between the minister and the faithful within the Church on the one hand, and the relationship between the Church and the world on the other. A Church that has an internal clerical structure will have clerical aims when presenting itself in human history. If the minister-community relationship is authoritarian and dominating, the Church will manifest itself to the world with claims of authority and dominance. If ministry consists in distance from the faithful, the Church will also try to establish distance from the world and its tasks instead of trying «to sum them up in Christ...». This parallelism is not developed in this work (which mainly tries to pay attention to the data from the sources), but I believe that enough elements appear to shed light on it.

——⬡——

Having established these three objective reasons, I will add a personal confession before addressing the subject. I was inspired to write these pages by a recent optimistic conviction. In spite of the painful, and oft mentioned, «ecclesial winter» (Karl Rahner) and in spite of the difficulties of this hour, I continue to believe in the creative possibilities given to the Church by its own sources —to which it always refers— and by the Christian fact —about which these same sources testify. What I will attempt to say is probably a truism: that ecclesial ministry (like the ecclesial community itself) is missionary. But this simplicity perhaps is encouraging. As maybe also another encouraging truism which will be the second thesis of this book: that God has not wanted to place useless or arbitrary limitations on the Church, but instead has wanted to open it creatively for the task that He has entrusted to it, which constitutes the Church's *raison d'être*. I continue to believe that Christianity still has a service to render and a word to say to human beings, if only the Church is willing to pay the necessary price in order to be able to proclaim that Word: to live for that mission which calls the Church and not for its own institutional interests. This is why the experience of the ecclesial ministry can still be positive and motivating.

In line with what has already been said, this book will consist of three parts: the Christian fact, the witness to that in the New Testament, and the shaping of it throughout history (especially in the first centuries). In other words: the Christology of ministry, the biblical theology of ministry, and the shaping of that ministry through a history that has been largely entropic and hardly creative. Many other issues (some apparently more «current» because more particular) will not be explicitly addressed here. But I do not believe that they will remain untouched.

In conclusion, there are two observations that I would like to make. This work was originally written for the publication *Revista Latinoamericana de Teología* when I was living in El Salvador. Even though this text differs slightly from that one, I consider this version the «official» one. Also, I would like to thank my colleagues Xavier Alegre and Josep Vives for their observations on the exegetical and historical aspects of the work, respectively, even though the responsibility for the statements made here is only mine.

Prologue to the Present Edition

For reasons I will now mention, the second edition of this work had been post-poned *sine die* when *Convivium Press* asked me for it to mark the Year for Priests. The previous introduction seems to me to highlight that opportunity: the Year for Priests coincided with and perhaps was motivated by one of the saddest periods in Church history: the scandal of child abuse by a good number of the clergy. Benedict XVI has had the courage to acknowledge these scandals, to de-clare that he felt ashamed, and to ask for courage and truth in order to elimi-nate these scandals once and for all. Some analysts of this terrible phenome-non (like the Australian Bishop Robinson who investigated this for the Church in his country) declared that the scandal was not only a problem of sexuality: it was also and perhaps primarily a problem of *power*: the absolutization and al-most divinization of those so-called priests who many times presented a strange sacred halo to the child who, more than anyone, was incapable of resisting. In my own pastoral experience I have known a similar case of a girl, not a child, very religious but with a simple faith, who felt shattered by having to reject cer-tain advances from her pastor, «a representative of God». I do not mean that it was the same as Abraham's sacrifice in the *Bible* but it was similar and the solu-tion to the dilemma did not come about until she demystified the figure of her parish priest realizing he was not a representative of God but a servant of the community and that what he intended to do with her was definitely not a serv-ice to the community. In the end the fundamental thesis that emerges from this historical study is that the ecclesial ministry is not about power, dignity, superiority and remoteness, but rather about service, surrender, sameness and nearness.

The reason for the delay in the second edition was that I wished to add a new chapter comparing the ecumenical «Lima Document» agreement about eccle-sial ministry, with the texts of the Council of Trent. But not only the «dogmatic» texts found in Denzinger, but also the «reform» texts of the same Session 23 of that Council. Because in Trent something happened which was also to be re-peated in part at Vatican II. As in Vatican II the Constitution «On the Church in the World» (*Gaudium et Spes*, GS) contains implicitly an ecclesiology which com-pletes the Constitution *Lumen Gentium* (LG) about the Church, so also in Trent many reform decrees contain an implied theology which completes and can-not be separated from texts considered to be dogmatic. Unfortunately, the de-crees on reform were very little taken into account (the resistance to Vatican II is not a thing of today only[1]), and this meant that the theology they irradiated did not influence theological reflection on ministry. I will give only a couple of examples: Canon 1 *De Reformatione* of Session 23 states that «it is *by divine precept* enjoined on all, to whom the cure of souls is committed, to know their own sheep, pasture them with preaching… and by the example of their lives and *to have a fatherly care of the poor and of all other distressed persons*». Canon 18 of that same Session, which deals with the establishment of seminaries, legislates that «the Council wishes to choose for them *principally the children of the poor, though without excluding those of the wealthier*». And Canon 16 of Session 23 reintroduces Canon 6 of the Council of Chalcedon which prohibits ordaining those who do not belong to a concrete church in a city, town or monastery[2]. All these cases are not simply about practical advice but about theological presuppositions that qualify and complete the texts in Denzinger. Because the fatherly care to the destitute and the preferential option for the children of the poor to the ministry suppose a turn-around in the association of such words as dignity, holiness and remoteness that figure so much in the imagination of the faithful in relation to presbyters. I cannot help recalling what happened many years ago in a most wonderful priestly ordination in a dump in Asuncion, Paraguay. The angry protests of some in the «hierarchy» who considered this «an insult» to the dignity of the priesthood made me wonder if when Christmas arrived those same ones would not make a similar protest against Jesus of Nazareth for being born in a stable and thus lowering the dignity of God himself. Fortunately, such declarations did not take place. But they would not have lacked arguments…

The fact is that I did not have time to research and write that new chapter and today, given my age and diminished health, I do not expect to do so.

Finally, perhaps I should add that what inspired me to write that unfulfilled supplement was the following occurrence. This book came out for the first time at the beginning of 1989. In July of that same year, the provincial of the Jesuits of Cataluña, at that time (Oriol Tuni) showed me a confidential note sent to him

---

1 In Spain, Archbishop Carranza spent 17 years in the prison of the Inquisition because of the animosity of the Inquisitor Valdés, who preferred to reside in Court instead of in his diocese as Trent had ordered… The reaction of the Inquisitor was to «find» Lutheran errors in Carranza's catechism, which today is considered impeccable. Another example of a frequent *modus operandi* in all conservative mentalities of our Church.

2 Chalcedon even declared these ordinations invalid. Trent only said «*nullus in posterum ordinetur*». Cf. ALBERIGO G., *Conciliorum oecumenicorum decreta*. Barcelona: Herder, 1962, 66 and 725-726. It is scandalous that our Church today falls short of this norm or to hypocritically tolerate ordaining bishops to non-existent dioceses («*in partibus*»).

from the Spanish Conference of Catholic Bishops expressing «a serious pastoral concern» with regards to my book. The Bishops' note admitted that the book was basically orthodox and they were not challenging it on that ground. But they did fear that it «would not encourage many vocations» but just the opposite… It occurred to me that I could respond with a certain irony, making use of classic scholastic distinctions: it will not raise vocations to the priesthood of Aaron, granted; to the priesthood «according to Melchizedek» is yet to be seen. I asked the Provincial if he wanted me to compose a response or clarification. He said it was not necessary since the letter was private, and he even hinted that he suspected that the note from the Spanish Conference of Catholic Bishops had been written (in case there were a complaint about the book to Rome and Rome would ask about it) to be able to say that they had already addressed the matter. Everything was left so and it seemed definitely over. However, in November of that same year, there was the killing of Ignacio Ellacuria, his companions in El Salvador and the two women Elba and Celina who had taken refuge in the residence of the UCA (about whom the press spoke less, even though my Central American brothers have always said that this had been the worst aspect of that incident). Inevitably, for days the media in Spain had the Jesuits as protagonists (five of them were Spaniards and the sixth one Salvadorian). Without doubt, it was excessive (I remember my own sleepless nights, unable to cope with the trauma, appearing as a sleepwalker in some press conferences). And there is a pretty strong suspicion that «someone» decided to shift the media spotlight by leaking the note from the Episcopal Conference about my book. With the typical oversimplification of the media, the Jesuits went from being the good ones to being the bad ones, or at least not so good, which was what it was all about. I reached a fairly coherent hypothesis about who could have tipped-off the media, and I remember I mentioned it to a high ranking church official who simply smiled and said that he knew nothing about it.

This was the episode, not very important in itself, which explains the vicissitudes of this book. If, because of the Year for Priests, it has seemed worthwhile to recover it, the reader has now access to it. I would only like to add that this edition by *Convivium Press* has some small corrections and additions, though not important enough to call this a «new edition» as they are not what I imagined at the beginning. The most important thing I was accused of was of denying the habitual theological formula about the activity of the presbyter «*in persona Christi*». I believe I can answer that it is not a matter of denying it but of casting it through a previous expression «*in persona Iesu*»: since there is no Christ without Jesus (as so many times is alleged tacitly within more conservative ecclesiastical circles). Speaking more clearly: the dignity of Christ is not given without following of Jesus, who turns this dignity upside down; nor is the dignity of the Risen One given apart from the Crucified One. And both, the Christological dignity and the following of Jesus, affect the whole community of believers, although the minister, as responsible for that community, is the first called to make real and bring alive these gifts. If later it is only the minister who pronounces the words of consecration it is not because he has some exclusive power the community lacks (at least in the first texts, as we shall see, the opposite was stated). It is simply because the *narrative* texts were, by their very nature, made to be read by one person only (contrary to the *acclamations* which by their very nature were made to be proclaimed by the whole community). It is not then in that supposed power where the Tridentine «essential difference» between the clergy and the laity should be established but in the representation of the whole Church proper to the ministry. This representation makes the sacrament true *action of the Church* and not the particular whim of some of its members.

But this controversial point seems to me the least important one in the following pages. The basic thing, I believe, is the thesis that never stops appearing in them that the Scriptures and the early tradition leave to the Church great liberty in relation to its structuring; furthermore, there are also some examples in the search for structuring those ecclesial services, taking into account the signs of the times and the needs of every hour and every historical situation. Given the needs of the present time, it seems to me that this dual thesis is not without significance. And I believe that to forget this, and to hold on tightly to what is not «God's commands but human traditions» (Mark 7:8) is one of the factors that have contributed to the loss of the spirituality of service inherent in the ecclesial ministry, with the risk of making it into a functionary career role.

José Ignacio González Faus
March 2010

The priesthood of Jesus and the non-priesthood of priests

The starting point for any reflection on the ecclesial ministry should not even be the structure of the early New Testament communities, but something closer to the roots: *the theology of the priesthood of Jesus Christ.*

Indeed, that theology had to be formulated during the time of the New Testament and in clearly polemic conditions. After a conspicuous and careful absence of the word «priest» in all of the New Testament, the *Letter to the Hebrews* appears vindicating that title but with these conditions: a) *only* for Jesus, b) and in a *new* way, which, c) supposes the *end* of any priesthood.

All the data seem to indicate that the *Letter to the Hebrews* is addressed to some Christians discontented by what they considered the «excessive secularity» and lack of «splendour of worship grandeur» in Christianity. It is probable that the recipients were the Christians of the community in Rome, whose «Jewish» origins (not Pauline) are considered nowadays a fact sufficiently established. In any case, they were disappointed Christians, who today would have something of «Lefebvrians», whose unhappy situation made them yearn for the whole religious ritual of the Old Testament. But the author of the Letter, far from accepting these demands, explains to his addressees:

a) that the liturgical grandeur of the Old Testament was pure empty shadow: «image and shadow» (8:5; 9:9,23; 10:1);

b) that what could have been there of good will or good intentions has been realized by Jesus in an existential and non-ritual way expressed with words such as «consummation» (2:10ff; 5:9; 7:19,28; 10:1,14; 11:40), «seated at the right hand» (1:3; 8:1; 10:12) and «enter into heaven» (4:14; 8:1; 9:24);

c) and that for them opens up in this way the possibility of a «new» covenant which consists not in the offering of ostentatious gifts, but in the donation of their lives. That is why the *Letter* introduces exhortations throughout its exposition and concludes with a long invitation to journey on and persevere.

It is necessary, therefore, to more thoroughly develop the theological systematization (or at least the outline of it) by which the author of *Hebrews* presents these conclusions. The first part of our work will be dedicated to that.

It is a well-known fact that studies of Albert Vanhoye constitute a necessary point of reference and almost a final word on this subject. His work will have a strong presence here, but in order to avoid an accumulation of citations, I will avoid constant references to his research[1].

---

1 Above all I have used *Situation du Christ* (Paris: Les Editions du Cerf, 1969); *Sacerdotes antiguos, sacerdote nuevo según el Nuevo Testamento* (Salamanca: Sígueme, 1984); plus the following

The Incarnation of God: culmination of all «religious» and Old Testament priesthood

Summarizing as much as possible, the priesthood, as a religious and Old Testament phenomenon, can be described with the four following traits:

a) a *ritual* consecration to God,

b) which made the consecrated one a *participant* in Divine Holiness,

c) and thus *enabled* them to appease God with sacrifices and to obtain from God blessings for humanity,

d) and in this way gave them a special «power» that *separated* them from the non-priests and served to make the Divinity transparent to them[2]. This power before God impacted, therefore, in power before the people.

History shows how this power before the people is protected and kept afterwards through numerous religiously justified human institutions: the «caste» system or the priestly family (the tribe of Levi), the systems that make this honor non-transferable so as to guarantee that it will belong only to those chosen by the Divinity, etc.

But these institutions are logical not only because of a possible desire for religious purity, but also because, in fact, the type of priestly power that we have described brings with it, everywhere, an assortment of *material* advantages. Paul recognizes the right of the Old Testament priests to «live from the altar» (1 Cor 9:13). Aristotle states that metaphysics could develop in Egypt because there the priests had their living needs sufficiently assured. In another context, whoever visits the pyramids of Teotihuacan in Mexico, will find that the best preserved ruins are the houses of the priests (the ones nearer to the pyramid) precisely because they had the best construction…

Here there is an intrinsic and constant danger of going from one type of logic to the other.

---

academic notes: *Textus de sacerdotio Christi* (Roma: PIB, 1969) and *De Epistola ad Hebreos Sectio Centralis* (Roma: PIB, 1966). See also SMITH J., *A Priest Forever* (London: Sheed and Ward, 1969) and KLAPPERT B., *Die Eschatologie des Hebraerbriefes* (Munchen: Kaiser Verlag, 1969). See also Chapter 3 («la revolución en el culto») of my book: *El rostro humano de Dios*, 2nd edit., (Santander: Sal Terrae, 2008).

2 Perhaps it is worth noting that this system of «separation» has an inherent logic. That is, it is assumed that God's holiness consists much more in God's distance from us than in God's Mercy. From this assumption, the religious experience of God's holiness and human sinfulness confirms the idea that it is only in «separating yourself» from all of humanity that it is possible to approach God without dying. Hence, the innumerable Old Testament «purity laws».

After this description we should add, as a brief commentary, that *even today* numerous Christians would identify their priests in a similar light. This is a matter of some concern: it means that the appearance of the ecclesial ministry sounds more, *in fact*, like the Old Testament than the Gospel. And that even if theologians explain that «it is not that», this explanation remains misunderstood or hijacked by academia and for the faithful means much less than the «appearances» of the ecclesiastic life today.

Because the message of the New Testament is, precisely, that *those four data we have just given are the ones overcome by the Incarnation of God in Jesus*. This is why these four facts are the ones the author of *Hebrews* tries systematically to destroy throughout his work. Let us see how:

a) and b): To begin with, *a ritual consecration will never bring God closer nor envelop the consecrated one in Divine Holiness.*

This is a pointless attempt to make use of God, to «enter into heaven» or to place oneself «at the right hand» of God. It is as futile an attempt as the one of the tower of Babel which is only shadow and appearance. The proof of the vanity of such endeavor is, for the author of the *Letter*, the human weakness that continues to surround those mediators supposedly touched by the ontological Holiness of God. On this point, *Hebrews* expresses the same doctrine as 1Timothy 2:5 when it affirms that there can only be «also one mediator between God and men»: Jesus; and describes this mediator as *anthropos-Christos*. In other words, Jesus can represent all of humanity before God because he shares with them the same human nature (cf. Heb 2:14 and Gal: 3:19-20), but he can represent God before all of humanity because he is Anointed (*Christós*) with the fullness of the Divinity (cf. Heb 1:3 but also Col 2:9). And *there is no other possible mediation because there is no such human power before God*: it is God who «descends», and it is his Spirit who makes us «reach Him». And makes us reach Him not by our gifts but through his own gift of giving up our lives (cf. Heb 8:8-11; 10:16). Such is the importance and the depth of the claim made by traditional theology that, in Jesus, the priest was *at the same time victim*.

c) That is why, *the offerings of the ancient priesthood did not reach up to God nor, even less, did they please or satisfy him, or change his disposition toward humanity.*

That is why the same thing happens to them as to the law: in spite of their «goodness» they have ended up becoming pure powerless performance, superstitious and (in the worst case) even magical. Proof of this, for the author of

Hebrews, is that those priests always had to be repeating their useless offerings. The reason for this is that God, because of his Holiness and Transcendence, is not appeased or satisfied with the blood of animals, nor with the splendor of vestments, nor with the meticulousness of ceremonial rules. If something human can please God, it will be that human part which is the gift of God himself to the human person. And these are not the *rituals and the ceremonies, but the new heart of the human being*. What is ritual recovers its positive aspects as effect or expression of that new heart and never as the cause or the substitution of it.

And the place where that new heart acted and manifested itself was precisely in the life of Jesus delivered unto death. This was the most contradictory thing to a ritual sacrifice that could be imagined; something that did not have ritual offerings nor took place in a holy place, but «outside» (not only outside of the Temple, but also «outside of the holy city»). And something that in addition was a «legal punishment» for a presumed religious criminal. This, of course, is looking at the death from the human perspective. However, seen from God's perspective, that event was an act of total self-surrender, of self-gift made possible by the eternal Spirit of God who is absolute gift (cf. Heb 9:14).

d) Precisely because of this, *this form of priesthood does not give the mediator absolutely any power to be set apart from others.*

The mediator is no longer someone «midway between the two», only semi-divine yet also super-human, but on the contrary: because his essence is self-giving, this leads him to «share in all with his brethren» (Heb 2:14), made the same as them «yet without sin» (Heb 4:15). Here lies the sought-for holiness of the Priest which, in some way, reveals Divinity: in assimilation (or in the «Incarnation»), and, from it, in communion (common-union) instead of in separation (cf. Heb 2:17-5:10).

As a conclusion from what has been said, let us add the following swift reflection: any endeavor to overcome the present crisis of the ministry by way of a project of «clericalization», that is, through a project of *separation* (in title, in social *status*, in attire... or in any of those things that are not «sin» according to Heb 4:15), is an attempt which will not resolve the current crisis in the ministry, but will instead increase the feeling of pure «falsity or shadows of true realities» which the author of *Hebrews* was denouncing. This can make the Church more «ghetto-like», but less Church; more community like the Essene one, but less community of Jesus; more organization of people's superstitions, but less institution of the Incarnation of God. It is clear that «the habit does not make the monk» and, in this sense, it is somewhat different. But if you can set social *status* and, in this direction, care must be taken that all this set of external characterizations do not convert, in today's Church, into «those persuasive words of the human being» which Paul deliberately renounced, because they cover up the message and release the hearer from confronting the madness of the preaching of the cross (cf. 1 Cor 1). This is why, it cannot be argued either that the renunciation of that external *status* on the part of the ministers of the Church equals always and in all circumstances to «being ashamed of Christ». There are situations in which this can be the same as *being ashamed of putting the identity with Christ precisely at a distance* with respect to the abused and the deprived of social recognition.

2
The «Lay» Jesus Christ, the only priest

That is, broadly speaking, the systematization of the author of *Hebrews* in order to combat the religious and Old Testament notion of the priesthood. From this same conception, the author of the *Letter* dares also *to recover for Jesus* the title of «Priest». And he does recover it, but with the characteristics we will now mention:

1) Underlining the *«lay» character* which, by nature, corresponded to Jesus versus the priestly caste: «the one concerning whom these things were said belongs to another tribe, from which no one has officiated at the altar. For it is evident that our Lord was descended from Judah, a tribe with reference to which Moses spoke nothing concerning priests» (Heb 7:13-14). The priesthood of Jesus consisted in a particular believing way of living out his human existence, his «lay» existence. Not, of course, in a laity *no more*, but in a *way of living it*. The Church cannot therefore search for the identity of the priesthood in a ritualistic withdrawal from that laity, but in its transformation towards the giving up of life.

2) Finding in the pages of the *Bible* the strange figure of *«another» priest* —Melchizedek—, our author converts the lack of information about him into a sign of Transcendence and uses it in this way to establish the principle that there «exists a priesthood of another class» (cf. 7:11), of another type. And this allows him to proclaim serenely that «the former regulation is set aside because

it was weak and useless» (7:18). In this way, Jesus can be called «Priest» but «of a different type»: «according to the order of Melchizedek» (5:10; 6:20).

3) And finally, reserving this new title of «Priest» for *Jesus only*, and never for the leaders of the community. In this way, the priesthood of Jesus denies, on the one hand, the «cultic» aspect of the old, affirming that there are no sacrifices to offer and what should be done is to commemorate, celebrate and update a human life which, by being life surrendered thanks to the Spirit (9:14), has come to be the one only sacrifice pleasing to God and the reconciliation of humanity with the Father. But in addition, the priesthood of Jesus denies also the aspect of «power» of the older priestly order: authority can only be service, and Jesus exercised his thenceforth: by the force of his truth and not by the dignity of a title of «Priest» which he lacked also. In the same way, when Peter and John started their ministry, the Jewish priests were surprised at the power of their word because they were unschooled, un-titled men (*idiotai kai agrammatoi:* cf. Acts 4:13).

———∞∞∞———

CONSEQUENCES

First. —From these facts, it will be logical, too, that, for the author of this *Letter*, what seemed to be the specific task of the priesthood, that is, the sacrifice (*thysia*), *should change its meaning too*. Our author will not reject completely this concept; he will recover it, but also «according to a new order». And using that allegoric capacity he possesses abundantly he will leave an open door in order to relate that new order to «the bread and the wine» (cf. Jn 14:18, alluded to in Heb 7:1). The author, naturally, does not force his allegory so that «bread and wine» will not be understood again as mere offerings of external gifts, since what he wants to underline is that the external gifts and the traditional habitual sacrifices do not nor can they please God, and so they do not solve anything for the human person (cf. Heb 7:19ff). While Jesus, in his new form of priesthood, holds a new type of sacrifice, which is the *donation of himself:* not «the blood of goats but rather his own blood» (Heb. 9:12).

> We will not develop here —though we will mention it— how from this last phrase one can develop the formula of «bread and wine» that our author so subtly presents in his allegory. From the references to donation of self and of his own blood (9:14,12), bread and wine cease to be mere *external* gifts and become ancient symbols of a way of being human: sharing needs (the bread) and communicating joy (the cup). When,

later on, the Church will talk about them as «the body» and «the blood» of the Risen Jesus, the Church will not be referring merely to the solid and liquid components of the human body, but to the *person* (the meaning of «body» in Semitic culture) and the *life* (the meaning of «blood» in Semitic culture) of the Lord Jesus. The person and the life of Jesus are the human need shared and the joy communicated to humanity. That is why God makes himself *truly* present there, and the Church has had a believer's fine instinct in all the arguments about the real presence in the Eucharist, even at those times when it perhaps lacked sufficient philosophical categories to express that presence. Here we can also see the depth of the classical thesis (mentioned earlier) that in this type of priesthood and sacrifice Jesus is *at once priest, victim and altar.* For the Levitical or religious priesthood, this would involve a contradiction! But this apparent contradiction highlights the destruction of the traditional concept of «priesthood».

Second. —Precisely because of this, the author of *Hebrews* will be coherent in his way of thinking and will urge the faithful —in the small practical section at the end— to «not neglect to do good and to share what you have; God is pleased by sacrifices (*thysiai*) of that kind» (Heb 13:16). For the Christian —thanks to Christ— worship has been uprooted from the ritual to a certain way of living the existential (compare Heb 13:16 with 7:27). The author warns his listeners that this must endure, even when it involves «to go to Him outside the camp, bearing His reproach» (cf. 13:13).

Third: —As can be seen, the meaning of the word *thysia* has changed completely. And only through this change can it be recovered, because this word, which in the Old Testament appears more than four hundred times, is only found twice in the gospels, spoken by Jesus and in both instances to undermine it (cf. Mt 9:13 and 12:7)[3]. Nonetheless, the theology of *Hebrews'* author is not unfaithful to Jesus: it has simply known how to show (likewise Matthew with regards to the Law[4]) that Jesus' disavowal was not «to abolish the sacrifice but to fulfill it». It is rather the Old Testament which —without Jesus— abolishes itself, because «it has brought nothing to perfection» (Heb 7:19)[5]. To express this

---

3 The word also appears undermined in Mk 12:33. But now not in words of Jesus but from a scribe who has questioned him and offers it as a consequence of the teaching given by Jesus in his answer.

4 Cf. Mt 5:17.

5 «Consummate», «bring to perfection», «divinize»…translate the famous *teleiosis*, which expresses the ontological perfection of God. I have deliberately avoided citing here the texts in which this word appears, given the impossibility of a satisfactory translation. It is important to point out even if only in a footnote that with this word is best expressed that alleged «ontological divinity» that neither the priests nor the ancient religious rites had. And that, according to

superseding of the Old Testament, the New Testament will resort to the adjective *amomos* (without defect), which according to the Jewish ritual should characterize the lamb[6]: an offering *without blemish*, there is no other than life for others, life surrendered; and that type of offering is totally impossible for the human being[7]. This detail is what permits us to say now a last word about the relationship between the *Letter to the Hebrews* and the rest of the New Testament. As after all that has been said, the question arises whether the author of *Hebrews*, with his retrieval of the priesthood in order to apply it to Jesus, does not depart from the rest of the New Testament testimony. The author himself seems to be sensitive to this objection when he explains to his listeners that since they have become «children», he must give them milk and not solid food (5:12).

3

A New Priesthood, unique and unrepeatable: true reality of all former shadows

In spite of the clear difference of languages, *Hebrews*, in essence, does not contradict the rest of the New Testament with its skillful recovery of the title «Priest». Rather, it has clarified things with some approaches which before perhaps had not been so explicit and cutting. Speaking of Jesus, Paul prefers to repeat the more secular expression «gave himself up». But Ephesians 5:2 calls the donation of Christ «gift and sacrifice (*prosfora kai thysia*)». And from there Paul can exhort Christians to convert *their persons* (no other external gifts!) into a «holy sacrifice» (cf. Rom 12:1, where *hagios* could be equivalent to *amomos*—«without blemish»— in the classic Old Testament expression). Paul will consider his own surrendering to the apostolic work as «sacrifice and liturgy» (*thysia kai leitourgia*,

---

Vanhoye, *teleiosis* translates precisely the expression «to fill one's hands» (*mille-yad*) which was used to designate the Old Testament consecration of priests. I argued the same point in *La humanidad nueva*, (Santander: Sal Terrae, 2000), 61-62 and 150-152.

6 This adjective can be found in Ex 29:1, Lev 1:3, 10;4:3;5:15, as well as in Ez 43:22… The strange thing about this word is that, in spite of translating a Hebrew word which refers to moral and religious purity (*tamim*), the Septuagint has used it, above all, for the *ritual* offering. As if expressing in this manner the search for apath (failed) for the impossible purity of the human person before God.

7 Heb 9:14 («offered himself without blemish») and 1 Pt 1:19 («a lamb spotless unblemished, Christ») apply the word to the work of Jesus Christ. From Jesus Christ, 2 Pt 3:14 will offer it as a program for Christians. The Pauline *corpus* will do the same(Eph 1:4; Phil 2:15; Col 1:22), always as the work of Christ or of God.

Phil 2:17), and even when acknowledging a gift from the Philippians, he will dare call it, in one of his affectionate outpourings, a «sacrifice pleasing to God» (4:18).

These few texts are, however, sufficient to affirm that Paul and *Hebrews* agree on the *existential* character of what the ancient sacrificial ritual has been transformed into (after Christ's self-giving). The only difference is that Paul, for this same reason, does not give the title of «priest» to the Jesus who offers himself, while the author of *Hebrews*, for the same reason, does. *Hebrews*, then, converts to «priesthood» what Paul had called «sacrificial surrender». Sacral language is now fully retrieved for the existential, without it being possible now to contrast the «sacred» and the «existential».

We find totally coherent with this approach the following two New Testament data which, in the light of the above, recover now all their significance and all their depth:

3.1. Deliberately, the New Testament always avoids calling «priests» (or any other designation derived from the Greek word *hiereys* or the Hebrew word *kohen*) the leaders of the Christian community, starting with the Apostles themselves. Not without difficulty, but with absolute decisiveness, the New Testament creates from scratch a new lexicon, derived from the existential, «profane», world, and not from the religious-ritualistic one: the sent ones (*apostoloi*), supervisors (*episkopoi*), servants (*diakonoi*), leaders (*hegoumenoi*) or simply «those who give a hand» (*kopiountes*)[8]. All this linguistic effort clearly shows two things: a) that the Church has to have, and always had its leaders; but b) those leaders have nothing to do with the religious fact of «priesthood», but with the existential fact of the life, given up unto death, of Jesus. In any case, as we will see, if there is something «priestly» in the New Testament, it is the life of the community that flows from Jesus Christ.

3.2. In line with this, the New Testament language, which never refers to the group of leaders as «priestly», does instead refer to the group of believers or followers of Jesus as «priestly» because by their baptism they are «called» to reproduce in themselves Jesus' life-offering. This occurs only twice in the New Testament. *Hebrews* had not dared to do it, perhaps because the Old Testament material it used for calling Jesus «Priest» had been the *individual* figure of Melchizedeck (personified also in the allusion to the King in Psalm 110). But

---

8 The orientation of this language is perfectly clear in Hebrews 12:15 where the natural concern or responsibility of *every Christian* for the community is labeled «episcopal».

other passages in the New Testament do because they find validation for this in the allusion in Exodus to a priestly *people*. And so the book of Revelation will speak in two instances of a «kingdom of priests» (1:6, 5:10; cf. also 20:6) and the *First Letter of Peter* which probably proceeds from Rome (where perhaps the *Letter to the Hebrews* was destined, as we mentioned before), maintains a coherence of language which seems deliberate and, if Rome were the recipient of *Hebrews*, it would permit us to speak of «a lesson well learned». 1 Peter calls the Christian people «priestly» in that «as living stones are being built up» and, in this way, offer to God, through Jesus Christ, «the spiritual sacrifice (*thysia*)» (cf. 1 Pt 2:5-6). But a bit later, speaking and exhorting the leaders of the community, among which the author includes himself, he does not call them «priests» but simply «presbyters» (1 Pt 5:1-4).

CONCLUSION

It is reasonable to conclude, then, that *the truly «priestly» dimension of the Church is not found in the ecclesial ministry (nor coincides with it), but in the life of Jesus communicated to the believer.* The priesthood of the faithful (cf. 1 Pt 2:5) is to give up part of their own life to build community[9]. This idea reinforces the claim made by many exegetes that the First Letter of Peter is in fact a *baptismal* address.

If we now take a look at our present historical moment, we must acknowledge that in this matter, the ecclesiastical language of today shapes a whole linguistic world that is contrary to the New Testament. At best, today it is usual to speak of Jesus Christ as «High» Priest, but not as *Only* Priest. With this we have ended up with a conception that sees the priesthood of Jesus not as something new which surpasses the ancient one, but as *one more particular instance* (even though the most sublime) of a universal concept of priesthood which, even after Jesus, remains untouched (and even confirmed). With this also, the additional uses of the word «priest» have ended up expressing, *in fact*, «other realizations of this general, universal concept of priesthood» more than the possibility of participating in the given life of Jesus by the surrender of the Christian's own life, made possible by the Spirit of Jesus.

---

9 Needless to say, in this sense it has a clear application to the «Builders of the community» who dedicate not a part but their whole life. See what we will say later in the transition to part two.

And, since this is latent unconscious in our Church, it is impossible to recover the «priesthood of the faithful» and its basis in Baptism, in spite of well-intentioned exhortations and proactive efforts to do so. But these exhortations are useless because they come up against an unconscious mentality contrary to the New Testament.

The assessment of this first part fits in three points: a) only *Hebrews* recovers the word priest, transforming and applying it merely to Jesus; b) the New Testament recovers, transforming it too, the word «offering» (*thysia*), which *Hebrews* does also though with less intensity, and c) the New Testament recovers the adjective priestly for the believing community, not for its leaders[10].

4

The Christian outline: the most profound fidelity within the obvious break-up

In closing, let me expand on something which has already been suggested and constitutes an important point in the theology of the *Letter to the Hebrews*. While carrying out his «revolution» and disavowing with such radicalism the religious, fact of the priesthood (including the Old Testament priesthood), the author of *Hebrews* does not believe that he is being unfaithful to the Old Testament, instead he believes he is fulfilling it. This is a decisive factor of any Christology: Jesus fulfills the Old Testament in the midst of an apparent break from it[11]. The argument in the *Letter to the Hebrews* returns repeatedly to this way of thinking by juxtaposing type and antitype, shadow and reality, announcement and fulfillment, etc., etc. But even better than the wording of the *Letter*, this same idea is formulated in a happy phrase by A. Vanhoye: «the Old Testament as revelation announces the end of the Old Testament as institution»[12]. We are at the heart of the fact of Jesus Christ, of his titles —which are applied to him chang-

---

10 In contrast, the evolution of the later Church will recover the term priest for the president of the Eucharist: as he does not offer created gifts but the life itself of Jesus delivered unto death. That is legitimate but it is important not to forget that the ones who offer the Eucharist are *all* the persons present (the Roman Canon already said: «*ipsi tibi offerunt*»). But then, as all the ecclesial ministries began to be absorbed into the Eucharistic presidency, they unduly acquired priestly character and thus were made sacred.

11 See, for example, what I say about the Messianism of Jesus in *La humanidad nueva*, (Santander: Sal Terrae, 2000), 252-257. Jesus is the One-hoped for who destroys all hopes.

12 VANHOYE A., *Sacerdotes antiguos, sacerdote nuevo según el Nuevo Testamento* (Salamanca: Sígueme, 1984), 197.

ing their meaning— and of his salvific mission, which gives life going to the depths through death.

It will be important never to forget this principle, because later, in thinking about our present situation, we will see how this principle has a certain applicability to the Church too. Although the Church is not now the Old Testament, neither is it yet the absolute fulfillment of the Promise. That is why it is fitting to say also of the Church that «the Church as revelation announces (not its end, but) its perpetual reform as institution». And this will be fundamental not only for the current problem, but, above all, for the total —and not Pharisaic— fidelity of the Church to the God of Jesus Christ. In this the sin of the Church can also resemble the sin of Israel: to cling to its own materiality and not know how to recognize the Jesus who comes to give it fulfillment in an apparent destruction of that materiality.

This so important principle can also account for the dynamic unity of the New Testament, in the midst of its proven plurality which we will now again perceive. So, Paul and James can seem to be contradictory in their formulations about Abraham or about justification by works. But the striking thing is how Matthew, starting from a spirit we could call «James-like» (because of the importance of the works), reaches positions of the disavowal of the law which are very linked to Paul, and how the writings of John, starting from a very Pauline spirit (anti-Judaic), arrive at «James-like» positions of the appreciation of ethics. The New Testament is the interaction between those pluralities and the totality of those partialities.

5
Transition to Part Two

Once we have established with all its radicalism the Christological doctrine on the priesthood, we must tackle an objection that could be formulated thus: the doctrine in the *Letter to the Hebrews*, precisely due to its polemical character, is excessively one-sided. It can be compared with some of Paul's controversial statements about the «exclusivity» of the cross or the «exclusivity» of faith which Paul later completes or qualifies with his own conduct or in less controversial moments.

In the case of *Hebrews*, the one-sidedness consists in an assertion not adequately «balanced» of the eschatological character of the Christian fact (the writer, at times, seems to think that sin in the Church is not possible anymore![13]). However, Christianity does not only affirm the «already» of eschatology but also its «not yet». The harmonization of both statements is one of the fundamental theological problems and, as I have already commented in Christology, it can authorize a certain *recovery* of past realities, provided that such recoveries do not involve a *relapse*[14].

In the context of the «not yet» of eschatology, the claim can be made that the immediacy of the fact of Christ requires other apparent mediations, but not because Christ's mediation, which has definitely joined our «flesh and blood» (Heb 2:14) with the «passing through the heavens» and the «sitting at the right hand of the Father» (Heb 8:1), was not definitive, but because of the lack of ability of human beings to grasp that fullness from the dimension of their concrete temporal history.

Putting it more simply, or perhaps more psychologically: even after Jesus Christ, the community still needs servants, the people need *witnesses*; and will tend to make them sacred, to turn them into «ontological bridges» between God and human beings and, therefore, into «priests» according to the old meaning. It is clear that people need external, solemn and ceremonial expressions and tend to magnify them and make them sacred. We must accept it, but understanding that this is a need of the *human psyche* and not an exigency of the «psychology» of God. Maybe it is pedagogically required by the human being, but not by the worship due to God. To clearly understand this would mean that the «recovery» of the superseded false mediations would not become a «relapse» into them or a return to the Old Testament. It must be a recovery which does not absolutize those pseudo-mediations but which is fully conscious of their temporary and provisional nature.

It is to the Church's merit through history to have understood this need of human beings and to have had the appropriate pedagogical understanding with it. But the pedagogical understanding would be distorted if it became renunciation since it would imply the relapse into the Old Testament and a tacit emptying of Jesus and his Christological significance. This danger has threatened

13 Cf. 6:31 and 10:26-31.
14 See GONZÁLEZ FAUS, *La humanidad nueva* (Santander: Sal Terrae, 2000), 150-151.

Catholicism many times: for example, even now we can remember many «catholic» lectures on Hebrews 5:1ff which understood this text as a description of the priesthood of Jesus Christ, when in truth it is a description... of the type of priesthood nullified by Jesus Christ! Oddly enough, the Christological part was employed in these lectures as a subtle excuse to go back to the Old Testament. In this same line of argument it is also worth recalling the questionable definition of «priest (*cura animarum*)» as «*alter Christus*», in which what was more curious and dangerous was that the «*alter Christus*» threatened to work as an excuse to exempt the minister from trying to be «*alter Iesus*»: it was the *dignity* of the Risen One more than the *human life* of the historical Jesus which the «*priest*» seemed to personify. This ideology of the «*alter Christus*» without the «*alter Iesus*» has been one of the reasons that has most distorted the exercise of the ecclesial ministry as well as one of the most serious causes of its current crisis[15].

As we will see now, the Church, because of its intra-historical —and not merely eschatological— reality *needs ministries*. The Church needs them because God, having incarnated in history, always respects the laws of history. But this ecclesial ministry does not have a foundation that is *immediately* theological or Christological (this would go against the oneness of the only Mediator and the unique Priesthood of Jesus Christ), but it does have an *ecclesiological* foundation. Sometimes there is a desire to recover this *immediate* Christological (or «priestly») character for the ministers of the Church, arguing that all the faithful are priests when able to direct their worship to God, but that the minister is so, too, manifesting the active presence of Christ Mediator (that is, of Christ Priest) in the lives of the faithful. But to this one must answer that the ecclesial minister can only manifest the active presence of Christ Mediator *by destroying his own mediating and priestly aspiration* (as this constitutes the Mediation of Jesus Christ). Otherwise, that attempted manifestation would insensibly become a *substitution.*

Also, in the Christian community there has to be someone who makes present the unique lordship of the Father and of Jesus (cf. 1 Cor 8:6), which is a fundamental and constitutive feature of the community, as the community of faith is no longer owner-of-itself, is not «democratic», but obedient. But this active

---

15 I make this claim, above all, at the *structural* level, without entering into the *personal* levels, where, evidently, there could have occurred (and in fact did occur) great holiness in the ways in which many priests have exercised their ministry.

presence of the one Lord will only be present if the minister destroys *his own name of lord,* or his own authority and not have others call him «father» (cf. Mt 23:7-11). Hence the tendency in the New Testament to avoid not only the concrete term «priest» but others like «hierarchy» and «power» (*eksousia*), for those responsible for the Church. Since, otherwise, again with the excuse of manifesting, they would really be supplanting. In fact, this is what happened not infrequently in the recent past: the priest was a priest through Christ, undoubtedly, but *in addition to* Christ; people saw him as representative *of God,* etc. This was why they were *separated* from all the rest, whereas the mediating function of Jesus Christ is realized in his «total assimilation» to his brothers (cf. Heb 2:17). So if we wish to speak of the visibility of the presence of Christ in the life of the faithful it is better to do so with the New Testament language of *reconciliation*: «God, who reconciled us to Himself through Christ and gave us the ministry of reconciliation» (2 Cor 5:18ff). *The ecclesial ministry is a service of reconciliation which incarnates the reconciliation of the world with God. It is a creative task of communion and of community which reflects the communion of the world with God. And because of this it is a missionary task.*

In other words, the ecclesial minister is not now simply or by his own status, a person «of God» or an «*alter* Christus», rather he is a believing «person for the community» and, precisely because of this and through this, a person of God and an imitator of Jesus Christ. In this way, the necessary ministry in the Church of Jesus Christ would be the *actualization* of the priestly character of the people as a fruit of the priesthood of Christ: it is at the service of that priesthood of the faithful and not against it or in competition with it. That actualization is an *active* memory: so what was later called the «triple office» (to teach, to govern, and to sanctify) consists in actualizing and building a «people of kings, holy assembly, and priestly kingdom».

We can say, then, that because the community needs men that is why God calls. On this point the ecclesial ministry can be connected to the call Jesus made to some in particular. This is why it is convenient to highlight (in the simplest analysis of that call) two features of it: a) it has to do with Jesus as «guide» or Lord and, therefore, it implies a following of his ministry, of his *kenosis,* of his life given over to the Kingdom of God… and b) this call is made concrete (more than by presiding over worship) by «fishing men». I have emphasized at other times that this «*fishing*» is not quantitative but qualitative, and can be assimilated to the concept «*teleiosis*» in *Hebrews* (consummate perfection): to bring out the best human realization in each believer with his or her conditioning factors and history[16].

According to all that has been said, the thesis of this work will be that the *contemporary historical moment seems to demand —and permits— a surpassing of that «relapse into the Old Testament»* (which the *Letter to the Hebrews* fights), *without ending up, on the other hand, in a communitarian eschatologism* —impossible because one-sided— *but in the call of Jesus and in the Christological fact.*

But, to specify the possibilities of recovering the Christological fact, it becomes necessary to explore now a little bit more the testimonies of the New Testament and the life itself of the Church. In other words, it is necessary to consider whether what the New Testament and the tradition permit and demand of the Church is consistent with what seems to be the imperative of our historical moment.

---

16 It is noteworthy that while Mk 1:17 uses the expression *alieis* (literally fishermen, referring to the profession of those who were called), Lk 5:10 changes the expression to *dsôgrôn* which means more to rescue, revive or to take *alive*: from now on you will be rescuing men.

The «Builders of Community»: Information from New Testament Ecclesiology

We have just stated that, even though —properly speaking— the Church does not have «priests», it does need however ministries: it needs functions that guarantee the healthy Christian life and discipleship of the community. We have also said that Jesus left the future Church his call, that is: the Apostles and their mission. In this fact converge not only a historical-theological reason (i.e., that *all* historical communities need this type of functions, and that the Church is not excluded from the laws of historical communities), or just a reason that «refers to Jesus», but also a positive reason: *the New Testament testifies to the fact that in the early Church such ministries existed.*

If, as we have just seen, the New Testament Church desperately looked for lay and not priestly names for these functions it is because there existed realities that had to be named. The real problem for today's Church is whether or not it can ascertain *how* these ministries *worked* and what there is in these ways of functioning which is *normative* for the Church.

This is a properly historical problem in which the systematic theologian must pay respectful attention to the research data, as theology does not have authority to ignore this type of mediations, and the Spirit, who has established them, does not seem willing to permit it either.

1

Obscurity and conflict in history inherent in the Church

Despite the complexity and variety of exegetical science, there is one first thesis we can establish today as guaranteed by New Testament exegesis. It could be formulated thus: precisely because Jesus only left to the Church the Apostles and their mission, the New Testament *does not offer any single mandatory model* on how to structure the Church (and even less a model given by Jesus himself or by the Apostles). Rather, the New Testament provides various examples of how different churches were structured, in answer to the needs and demands of different historical moments. It is true that from those examples emerge some generic lines (or «guidelines»), but they never constitute a finished model for the Church.

By a simple verification of a «table of contents», it is easy to point out that the New Testament has preserved information about the community in Jerusalem, the Church in Antioch of Syria, the Church in Corinth and some other Pauline

Churches, the Church in Rome to which was addressed one of Paul's letters (who knows if *Hebrews,* too, as we said before) and from which probably came the *First Letter of Peter* (and who knows if perhaps the «Pastoral» Epistles, as we will see later on)... It is not necessary to draw up an exhaustive list. What we want to establish now is that the information about all those communities allows us a glimpse of *diverse models* of structuring the Church and the ecclesial ministry.

We also find in the New Testament information about distinct eras. Some from the time when the Apostles were still alive; others about the time called today «sub-apostolic» (last third of the 1st century), and a few that seem to refer to the post-apostolic era. These epochal testimonies are also *diverse.* None can be considered normative and exclusive of the others; nor is there a «canon within the canon» even though the subsequent development, for historical reasons, led to the primacy of some of these models over others. But in their plurality all of them try to keep alive the Gospel of Jesus and faith in him. What happens is that they are marked by a thousand historical circumstances which go from *the needs of a particular situation* (like the need to open up to pagans what was imposed on the church of Antioch, or the dangers of loss of identity which seem to threaten the churches of the «Pastoral Letters»...), to *qualities of some particular especially strong personality* (as could be the prestige enjoyed by Paul or James, either among the Greek communities or in the early community in Jerusalem).

> Through this chapter we will enlarge on the conditioning produced by circumstances, which highlights both the diversity and the great creativity of the New Testament churches (and, of course, their disputes, too). For now, perhaps a subsection will be convenient to point out that the thesis we have just set out is an elemental fact scientific investigation considers today as already attained (the questioning of which would make all specialists smile). But on the other hand, it is a fact which clashes head on with the mentality—more so than with the words— of some of those responsible for the Church whose ecclesiological training ended many decades ago, and who (perhaps unconsciously thinking in self-defense) seem to believe that Jesus himself had left the Twelve Apostles a sort of «Ecclesial Constitution» or «Foundational Document» by which they were commanded to lay their hands upon a few «successors» (or bishops) who in turn would name their own helpers (or presbyters) also by laying hands on them and on others less important (deacons) to build in succession the process up to now...

In this way and by a deliberate decision of Jesus (*ius divinum*), the current structuring of the ecclesial ministry (bishops who ordain priests and deacons) would have been functioning, in an almost unchanged way, practically since the Resurrection of the Master. In this way, a *simply formal* concept of apostolicity is elaborated, consisting in the uninterrupted succession by the laying on of hands, from some Apostle until our present bishops, and which would constitute the *only* guarantee of true ecclesial character. It is also a known fact that Vatican II attempted to formulate this point with enormous caution and qualified the expression «*divina ordinatione*» which Trent seemed to apply to «bishops, priests, and deacons», applying to them the sufficiently vague expression «from ancient times», and leaving the *ius divinum* only for the ecclesial ministry in general[1]. But, even so, this is not the outlook that seems to prevail *when it is time to act* and to judge, but rather that of the Council of Trent.

In fact, that way of approaching the issue is extremely simplistic and simplifying[2]. As strange as it may sound to some (although totally coherent with the life of the historical Jesus), we must start by affirming that the Apostles did not have, prepared by the Master beforehand, the answer to any of the great problems that they had to face: they did have reference to Him, their coexistence with Him and the promise of being able to count on his Spirit «every day until the end of time».

The best proof of this assertion is provided by the first half of the *Acts of the Apostles*. The title of this book is unfortunate since —as is already known— it speaks very little of the acts of «the Apostles». Rather, the first half of the book recounts the birth of the first churches (that in Jerusalem and those of the Diaspora), with a significant role for Peter, while the second half is almost exclusively a narrative of Paul's journeys.

In my opinion, that first part of the book of *Acts* could be entitled, more accurately, something like «Book on Obscurity and Conflict in the infant Church». Obviously, it is trying to tell us that from this obscurity the Church will live on. But this narrative is transfixed by these two themes:

a) After the resounding initial success of the first preaching by the Apostles, the infant Church —which continues preaching with absolute conviction the salvation by Jesus Christ— begins to experience that it has no thought-out

---

1 Cf. LG 28, 1, with DS 76.

2 Cf. LOHFINK G., *La Iglesia que Jesús quería*, Bilbao: Desclee, 1986; ALEGRE X., «El movimiento de Jesús y las primeras comunidades cristianas» in *Misión Abierta*, 5-6 (1987) 28-57.

solutions to adopt when the first organizational problems emerge, such as: the admission of pagans, the break with the Jews, fanaticism of the converted Pharisees, imposition of circumcision and other rules of the Jewish law about food, etc.; the dilemma between keeping intact the number of the Twelve, because of its eschatological significance —which was the inclination at first of the Church of Jerusalem— or renouncing it in view of historical needs; the adoption as Apostle of «one untimely born» who did not meet the fundamental condition of being «one of the men who accompanied us the whole time the Lord Jesus came and went among us, beginning from the baptism of John» (Acts 1:22). For none of these problems (or similar ones) did the Church have previously programmed answers, so it had to solve them, as they arose, with creativity and faithfulness to the Spirit (more than to the letter) of Jesus and thanks to the daring charisma of some of its members. Moreover, if in some cases the Church believed to have established previous legislation (as the case we mentioned of the number Twelve for the Apostles), its decision was rapidly overcome by the dynamic of history.

b) In that creative task of responding to the challenge of history, the Church also faces the complication and unrest produced by the resistance of certain groups. First, the Jews, from whom they will end splitting; later (now inside the New Testament Church), the Christians who came from Judaism, or «converted Pharisees» (cf. Acts 15:5). As the Church opens up to the mission, first it will stumble on the resistance of the «Jerusalem curia», which lived awaiting Jesus' return more centered on itself and less geared toward history, but controlling —and sometimes hindering— all the missionary activity of the rest of the Church.

This perplexity and this resistance added further difficulties to the path of the early Church. Perhaps they also tempered it. But in any case, they provide us with the great lesson that always, despite the fact that the struggles became «very strong» (Acts 15:2, 6, cf. also 21:20-22), the Judaeo-Hellenist and the Jewish-Palestinian churches learned to avoid a total rift and completely break from one another. This is how the early Church managed to advance and taught us that in this human history there is no progress in any other way.

Fortunately, that early Church seems to have had, in the figure of Peter, a mediator sufficiently bold, while at the same time, patient and understanding. But one can imagine that for the Twelve it could not have been easy to accept that it was precisely the upstart and former persecutor, Paul, who would set for *them*, who had been with the Lord from of old, the path along which, in fact, the whole Christian mission would develop. About Paul we are expressly told that he «was baptized» (cf. Acts 22:16), but not that he was incorporated into the Apostolate by any special form of «ordination», as was the case with Matthias (the imposition of hands in Acts 13:3 seems to refer to a *concrete* mission and not to the Apostolate of Paul)[3]. And it is true that Paul did the impossible in order not to break with the Twelve because he considered that then his mission would be «in vain» (Gal 2:2); but the probing and conflicting manner in which events took place must not have been the expected one, as happens always when God entrusts a mission.

Perhaps this forces us to try to pin down a little more that notion of an «apostolic authority» previously established and purely formal, so to speak. Well, in my opinion, one should say that the concept of «apostolicity» resembles much more a concept of «balance», or a result of all those decisions and interactions, and not a preset juridical concept, known already by the Apostles when they began to preach and organize the infant Church.

This balance will show throughout our exploration of the New Testament. Now, after this comprehensive introduction, it is time to say a word about the structuring of the diverse New Testament churches in order to determine the content and form of the Church ministry.

2

The Johannine Communities: A Church without Apostolic Authority?

In order to connect with what we just said, we will begin the study of the New Testament with a group of later texts. And to contextualize the problematic situation with which these texts confront us, we will make a brief reference to our own ecclesial life.

When this book was being written, Edward Schillebeeckx had already published his work on the ministry, where he seemed practically to identify the notion of «apostolicity» with the «*sequela Iesu*», that is, with what constitutes the condition of possibility and the content itself of the sending of the Apostles by

---

3 At least according to Paul, he considered himself «an Apostle not from human beings nor through a human being but through Jesus Christ and God the Father who raised him from the dead» (Gal 1:1).

Jesus[4]. The Vatican's Congregation for the Doctrine of Faith was not satisfied with this concept of apostolicity and, in a document dated August 6th 1983, asserted uninterrupted succession as formal constitutive of apostolicity[5].

Without going into personal controversies, I think that the Congregation for the Doctrine of the Faith is not without reason in rejecting a *merely material* apostolicity identified with the following of Jesus. This was the objective of the assessment of Schillebeeckx's book. But I think that neither can we defend, against this concept, another *merely formal* authority, defined as pure successive transmission without any reference to the content of that succession, which is surely the following of Jesus. And I do not think that this point has been denied by the Congregation for the Doctrine of the Faith. The theological notion of «apostolicity» in its fullness contains both dimensions[6]. And that apostolicity is

4 Cf. SCHILLEBEECKX E., *El ministerio eclesial: Responsables en la comunidad cristiana* (Madrid: Cristianidad, 1983). I am fully aware of the fact that Schillebeeckx's position on the issue is much more complex than what my text suggests. However, what probably caused alarm in this point could have been phrases like: «Apostolicity means *primarily* the awareness by the community of their continuing Jesus' cause… *Therefore*, apostolicity includes, concretely: the apostolic proclamation of the message of Jesus, which is inseparable from his person and, thus, from his Death and Resurrection. The apostolic interpretation of the rejection and death of Jesus belongs to the essential nucleus of the gospel» (73, italics mine).

5 «*Apostolicitas Ecclesiae non ita intelligenda est ut omnes fideles sint Apostoli, etsi collective modo; nec ulla communitas potestate gaudet conferendi ministerium apostolicum, quod fundamental-iter ab ipso Christo Domino conceditur. Ecclesia igitur, cumse per Symbola apostolicam profitetur, praeter concordiam magisterii sui cum doctrina Apostolorum*, continuitatem exprimit numeris Apostolorum, ope structurae successionis effectam, *vi cuius mission apostolic usque ad consum-mationem saeculorum permanent oportet.*
Huiusmodi Apostolorum successio, qua Ecclesia tota constituitur apostolica, pertinet ad vivam Traditionem, quae inde ab initio in Ecclesia facta est atque esse pergit forma vitae ipsius Ecclesiae. Quare a recto tramite aberrant qui huic vivae Traditioni singulas Scripturarum partes oppo-nunt, exquibus ius adalias structuras deducere volunt» (III, 2).
The emphases are mine. The first paragraph summarizes the position of the Congregation for the Doctrine of the Faith though it does not state the exact content of the «*structurae successio-nis*»; we will assume that it refers to the imposition of hands done with that intention. In the second, the Congregation seems to concede that this position *is not derived from the Scriptures* (which it can even contradict) but derives from the Tradition of the Church. What is most sur-prising is that it seems to privilege the authority of the Tradition over that of the *Scriptures*. This point seems to require further research.

6 The merely formal conception of apostolicity suggests an ecclesiology which excessively sepa-rates the ministries from the community: the word church would be reserved only for the «hi-erarchy» and not for the whole community. But this is about a language (and a mentality) in which the ministry is not *outside* the community but *within* the community and pertaining to it. There is not (to use Lenin's language) a Church «in itself» and a Church «for itself» which would be the one truly deserving the name of Church. And in this sense it is possible to say that the Church is a democracy, or even more: it is a communion. Deep down, what are opposed in these languages are two ecclesiologies: the one assumed and taught by Vatican II, and the one that was reflected in the previous schemas prepared by the Roman Curia and which were re-

the basis of the ecclesial ministry because it *is the only thing that comes from Jesus.* Those two components may at some definite time supplement or compensate one another, but in the long run they must *be together.* Any pretension to a purely material apostolicity degenerates into division and in a multiplicity of sects (all of which will appeal to the «*sequela Iesu*» precisely in order to break away from the others). But also any appeal to a merely formal apostolicity degenerates into stagnation and the solitude of a «*rigor mortis*» where uniformity arises precisely from the lack of life and where Jesus' authority of truth is substituted by the human force of authority. In words of the New Testament, the merely material apostolicity, pure «*sequela Iesu*», tries to be a building with a «cornerstone» but without foundations (cf. Eph 2:20); while a merely formal apostolicity resembles a building carefully raised «on the foundation of the apostles and prophets», but without the cornerstone that is Jesus Christ (cf. Eph 2:20). It will now be convenient to offer two separate examples of both. And for that the trajectory of the Johannine communities is made to order.

2.1. THE FOUNDATION OF THE APOSTLES

In the so-called *Johannine writings* (Gospel and letters) we probably have a case of «material» apostolicity in which the absolute reference to Jesus and his following was what ended up giving them authority[7]. Present day exegesis converges increasingly on saying that immediately behind these texts there does not seem to be any Apostle, not even once can we find this word in them, a word so frequent in any of the other New Testament writings (except in the generic formulation of John 13:16). Its point of reference is simply Jesus and what gives authority in those communities is not the person of any of the Twelve, but that mysterious figure of the «beloved disciple» who maybe was not even a real person but the incarnation of the ideal of these texts, or maybe a leading figure in the community, who could be the «presbyter» author of the second and third Johannine letters, or the unidentified disciple in John 1:35-40. A figure to whom the community attributes in a special way the configuration of its tradition. But

jected by the Council's assembly. In my opinion the notion of apostolicity is greatly enriched from an ecumenical point of view in Chapter 9 of SULLIVAN A., book *La Iglesia en que creemos* (Bilbao: Desclée de Brouwer, 1995).

7 Cf. BROWN R., *La comunidad del dicipulo amado* (Salamanca: Sígueme, 1983); *The Epistles of John* (New York: Doubleday and Company, 1982). TUÑI J.O., *Jesús y el Evangelio en la comunidad joanica* (Salamanca: Sígueme, 1987). SCHNACKENBURG R., *El evangelio según San Juan* (Barcelona: Herder, 1980). ESTRADA J.A., *La Iglesia, ¿institución o carisma?,* (Salamanca: Sígueme, 1984), Chap. 4.

a figure whose identification with the apostle John is very much questioned today by historical criticism. *It is, therefore, «discipleship» which has made these texts part of the New Testament,* without any formal reference to «apostleship» (or, more exactly: only with the late reference of Chapter 21, added subsequently, even though also canonical, of course).

This, then, seems to raise what was objected of in Schillebeeckx. And in effect the ecclesiology of the Johannine writings is all made by «*sequela Iesu*», by the relationship of the individual disciple with Jesus and actualized in every moment by the Spirit, to such an extreme that the Fourth Gospel —as we know— rewrites the life of Jesus from the context of the life of that community[8].

And this relationship with Jesus is painted with the most powerful strokes of the whole New Testament (the vine and the branches; Jesus' knowledge of the Father —Jn 10:15—; the fullness of life of the Christian...). That is why it becomes the strongest (and most unifying) element amongst all the other features which shape the community and can be differentiating. If the phrase «*what unites us* is more than what divides us» were true in some cases it would be so most of all in the community of the Johannine writings. Since what does unite is the insertion of all the different branches in the one true Vine.

Such a relationship with Jesus is what will make «the disciple» be present at the foot of the cross of the Master (cf. Jn 19:25-26), there where all those entrusted with the «apostolic ministry» have already fled, according to the paradigmatic lecture by Urs von Balthasar[9]. It will also make «the disciple» *see more* than Peter and always reach faith before Peter does (cf. Jn 20:8; 21:7). There is no need to force things in order to perceive here a hidden criticism of the scheme of «authoritarian ministry» in the «Pastoral epistles» —to which we will refer later on—, as this scheme threatens the possibility that obeying authority will become more important than following Jesus (as the former assures and guarantees order in the community, while the latter could in some cases endanger it). On the contrary, in the Johannine scheme the only important thing is personal surrender to Jesus Christ, which is the only thing that makes a person Christian and cannot be prevented by anyone or anything. Precisely because of this one has the

8 Examples in TUNI J.O., *Jesús y el Evangelio en la comunidad joánica* (Salamanca: Sígueme, 1987), 36ff. Classic references are the expulsion from the synagogue of those who claimed Jesus as the Messiah, the conversion of the Samaritans, and the designation of the adversaries as «the Jews». These things have to do with the historical circumstances of the community and not with the time when Jesus lived.

9 VON BALTHASAR H. U., *Mysterium Salutis*, III, 2 (Madrid: Cristiandad, 1971), 215-217.

impression that the Johannine writings do not reflect any structured form of ecclesial authority: we do not find doctors, or prophets or ministers... not even «apostles», as we have already mentioned. There is only one Good Shepherd, all the rest are hired hands (Jn 10:11ff), though this does not negate the *interior* authority the «beloved disciple» exercised in that community. In other words: *the purpose of any ministry and of the whole of the ecclesial mission is that men and women follow and obey Jesus.* Where such obedience takes place, the ministry would become practically superfluous. If this is the purpose of ministry one could say that it is realized «*in persona Christi*», provided that it does not mean that the community follows the minister (in place of Jesus), but that the minister is the first follower obedient to Jesus. «*In persona Christi*» does not mean that the community follows the minister as Christ but that the minister is asked: «Do you love me more than these?»...

From this brief reflection on the ecclesiology of the Fourth Gospel emerge two very important and conflicting reflections:

a) Despite all that has been said, the Fourth Gospel was included in the «canon» of the New Testament, as we have already mentioned. Its reference to Jesus, so intense, made this possible.

b) But this entrance into the «canon» only took place *after* the Gospel had been modified by (or received the correct interpretation of) the Letters and Chapter 21.

Why was this qualification necessary? Because over time the Johannine community had the experience of how this reference to Jesus (whose capacity to unite seemed at the beginning more powerful that any disrupting force) could become at the same time a factor of division. Each one was susceptible of falsifying the same Jesus to whom all referred, filtering him more through their subjectivity than through the Spirit of Jesus. So almost immediately, through the eagerness to exalt him, «docetic» readings of Jesus appeared, to which the Fourth Gospel seemed to give support. Many well-loved disciples must have thought that anyone who did not present a docetic image of Jesus was denying his divinity, as did the Jews whom this Gospel opposed. Or it must have seemed to them that the conflict with the Jews (who had persecuted them) demanded a *total* break with anything to do with Judaism... And when this group of disciples felt called to impose their points of view (for love of Jesus, without doubt, but taking advantage of the egalitarian character of the community) the result was that the community itself was threatened. This led to a split in the community, as is shown in the so-called letters of John, in which each group felt justified by its love for and bond to Jesus to call the other «anti-Christ». This is why in those letters, curiously, the irreconcilable enemies are not «the Jews» of the Fourth Gospel anymore but the other separated brothers and sisters.

The appeal to Jesus and to the Spirit ended up being insufficient to prop up the Church because it was a «cornerstone without foundations» as we pointed out earlier. And probably (this is at least the opinion of Raymond Brown) a part of the community decanted towards Gnosticism while the other part of the community was saved —as is usually said— because it accepted integration into the greater Church: it accepted the «formal» authority (that of Peter), not without stating very clearly its conditions and limits: it is an authority that can only come from love; an authority that is not holy in itself, since he denied Jesus three times; an authority that does not graze its own flock but that of the Lord and that cannot dispose of nor fully integrate the mysterious figure of the «disciple», but must concern itself more with its *own* following… But, despite everything and in contrast with what was said in Chapter 10 about the one Good Shepherd, Peter is now entrusted with «grazing the flock». This seems to be the meaning of Chapter 21, which R. Brown considers not only a later addition to the Gospel but even subsequent to the three letters of John[10]. If in all the rest of the Gospel (Chapters 13, 18, 19 and 20[11]) the «disciple» was opposed to Peter with advantage, now, in this appendage, the community recognizes Peter's role.

In conclusion: the Johannine writings did not enter into the «canon» due to some «formal» apostolic authority that validated them but due to the «apostolicity» of its following of Jesus. This was expressed by the classical procedure of pseudonymia: they were given the name of the Apostle John and were accepted as apostolic writings. But *in the long run* they could not have made it into the New Testament without accepting at least a minimum of formal apostolicity. They confirm, then, as we earlier said that the apostolic authority from which the ministry arises is not something *merely* formal and juridical, but that it has a material content which is the «*sequela Iesu*». But in the long run merely

---

10 «It could represent the last phase of the Johannine writings» BROWN R., *Las Iglesias que los Apostoles nos dejaron* (Bilbao: Desclee de Brouwer, 1986), 120. But in his detailed commentary on the Fourth Gospel, *El Evangelio segun Juan* (Madrid: Cristianidad, 1979), Brown does not provide a date for Chapter 21.

11 The washing of the feet, the denials, the absence at the foot of the cross —save for the beloved disciple— and the visit to the empty tomb.

material apostolicity ends up degenerating into divisions and a multitude of opposing sects[12].

2.2. THE CORNERSTONE: JESUS

At the other extreme maybe it is not possible to find an equally pure example in the New Testament, among other things because, due to a lack of historical perspective, the notion of formal apostolicity was not then coined with the precision with which we discuss it now. However, it may be helpful now to recall the division that Paul faced in the Church at Corinth, where some saw themselves as belonging to Cephas, some to Paul, some to Apollos, etc. In this context of confrontation, Paul gives three very important criteria: a) the ministers (Paul, Apollos, Cephas, etc.) are only men and «no one should boast about human beings» (cf. 1 Cor 3:21); b) because of that, ministers are no more than «helpers in the faith» of each person, but the one who gives the faith is the Lord (cf. 1 Cor 3:5); and c) the Lord Jesus is in no way «given in exclusivity» (1 Cor 1:13). So divisions are not going to be solved by bidding to see «who commands more» but determining «to know nothing except Jesus Christ, and him crucified» (1 Cor 2:1). The community of the Fourth Gospel would have been glad to subscribe to this radical and controversial appeal which makes us see how «formal» apostolicity receives its content and justification from the connection with Jesus.

But if we want a purer example maybe we must move from the New Testament and make an early entry into Church history. And since it seems worthwhile I will recall a unique, swift example that deals with our question *from the highest level* of apostolic authority which is the authority of the ministry of Peter. The example comes from the decree *Haec Sancta Synodus* of the Council of Constance, formally ratified by Pope Martin v himself[13].

---

12 In the same vein are H. Fries' words in his famous work in collaboration with K. Rahner: «Apostolic succession in episcopal ministry is a *sign* of the apostolicity of the Church but is not apostolicity itself. History shows how there are bishops who can be left outside of apostolic succession, for example during the Arian controversy when it was not even sure that the majority of the bishops followed orthodox doctrine. This impression is confirmed when one reflects on the criteria and the conditions for the naming of bishops in the Middle Ages» *La union de las Iglesias. Una posibilidad real* (Barcelona: Herder, 1987), 128-129. See also what J. Roloff says in his commentary on the *Acts of the Apostles* (*Hechos de los Apostoles*, Madrid: Cristianidad, 1984, 90) about the convergence of witness and testimony.

13 See, above all, ALBERIGO G., *Chiesa Conciliare* (Brescia: Paideia, 1981). See also ULLMANN W., *The Origins of the Great Schism* (London, 1948); THIERNEY B., *Foundations of the Conciliar Theory* (Cambridge: Cambridge University Press, 1955). See also VOOGHT P. DE, «El conciliarismo en los concilios de Constanza y Basilea», in *El concilio y los concilios*, ed. ROUSSEAU O., (Madrid, 1962)

The situation in which the Church was placed by the Western Schism, in relation to our subject, could be presented thus: the defenders of a *merely* formal apostolicity will have to take into account the real possibility that the apostolic succession has been definitively broken and no less than for the Petrine ministry. What would happen if, in effect, the real Pope were the one called the Pope «of Avignon», who was succeeded by Pope Luna, Benedict XIII, whose succession was interrupted? What would happen would be this: the current popes would lack that purely formal apostolicity!

Now, history has been unable to establish a verdict about who was the real pope in that schism. And the Church prudently has also abstained from issuing a judgment. The arguments of the Cardinals who deposed Urban VI and elected the first Avignon antipope are not inconsiderable even though they are not indisputable. And the decisive issue is that in order to make a judgment we have nothing more than the testimony of those Cardinals. If they lied that is something that today we cannot know. In any case, as I have just said, the Church not only has declined to give a definitive verdict but also has never considered as schismatic those who denied obedience to one of the popes in order to give it to the other one, even though both popes had hastened to excommunicate the other and his followers, among whom —on both sides— there are even canonized saints.

The question remains: if indeed the *merely* formal succession was broken with Benedict XIII —which could historically be possible— how is this succession restored so as to legitimize the later popes? The answer is by the Council of Constance's decree of April 6th, 1415, which defined the authority of that same Council «for the eradication of the present schism and for bringing unity and reform to God's Church in its head and members», an authority which «all Christians, including the pope, are bound to obey», and which the Council exercised by deposing John XXIII in 1415 and Benedict XIII in 1417 (and in part also, although more gently, by persuading Gregory XII to resign). Therefore, although Pope Luna had formal succession, he was deposed permanently for a lack of *material* apostolicity, because by their stubbornness he and John XXIII departed from the real following of Jesus by prolonging the schism and putting their own personal claims before the good of the universal Church.

and his articles in *Istina* (1963), 57-86, and in *Irenikon* (1963) 61-75. See also DE VOOGHT *Les pouvoirs du Concilie et l'autorite du pape* (Paris, 1965). In addition, see JEDIN H., *Manual de historia de la Iglesia*, vol. IV (Barcelona: Herder, 1973). A clear and straightforward summary of the issue is found in KUNG H., *Estructuras de la Iglesia* (Barcelona: Estela, 1965), 265-310.

Here we have a case —perhaps the best one— which indicates how a merely formal apostolicity may not be sufficient when it lacks the content and the accompaniment of Jesus' mission. Even the advisors to Pope Martin v, who was elected by the Council of Constance, would recommend him to accept all of the decrees of the Council (in spite of the obligations to reform the Church which they imposed on future popes, which they ended up not observing) as the only way of definitely guaranteeing his own legitimacy. And so the decree *Haec Sancta Synodus* met the last legal requirement that is demanded today of a Council's decree: to be approved by the Pope[14].

The two examples that we have offered in these two sections are obviously *extreme cases.* In practice, formal apostolicity and material apostolicity are sufficiently united and it will not be necessary to use one against the other. But, in the extreme case where this unity were broken, we know that neither one can be used on its own against the other. Each one demands its complement.

And the proximity between both concepts of apostolicity helps to understand why the notion of apostolicity does not appear clearly established in the New Testament or at least fully established in all its documents nor in all the primitive churches. In normal times in the life of the early Church, the «*sequela Iesu*» functioned as a sufficient guarantee of apostolicity. At other times of crisis or conflict perhaps not: it will be necessary then to appeal to formal succession: and this is what the «Pastoral Letters» seem to do, as we will see later on. But this appeal, even though necessary, is not, in itself, a magical guarantee, as can be seen in other extreme cases. These criteria will be important to understand and study the rest of the churches of the New Testament. We will continue on, leaving well established that discipleship only is not apostolicity, but nor can we have apostolicity without real discipleship[15].

14 Cf. In ALBERIGO G., (*Conciliorum oecumenicorum decreta.* Barcelona: Herder, 1962, 246) the testimonies of Giovanni de Ragusa and Ludolf von Sagen. Still, when at the Council of Basel things started to go out of control and Eugene IV (Martin v's successor), thought of dissolving the Council, Cardinal Cesarini wrote to him saying that «if someone says that the decrees of that Council (Constance) are not valid, that person must also confess that the deposition of John XXIII as pope, made on the basis of those decrees, had no value. And if this was so, neither did the election of Martin v that took place when John was still alive. And, if Martin v was not a pope, then neither is your holiness…» The full citation is found in KUNG H., *Estructuras de la Iglesia* (Barcelona: Estela, 1965), 276.

15 Something similar could be said of another one of the texts of the early Church presented as decisive in support of purely formal apostolicity: I am referring to Book III of *Adversus Haereses* by Irenaeus of Lyons. Irenaeus does not attempt to make *pure* formal apostolicity into a *universal* criterion for apostolicity, but he builds instead an «*ad hominem*» argument in a moment of crisis when heretics appeal to the gospel of Jesus, claiming to have a better knowledge of this

Variety and creativity in the churches in the «Acts of the Apostles»

The hardship of the first steps of the Church, mentioned in the first part of this chapter, provides us with a series of concrete facts important for our study of the ecclesial ministry. Because little by little it will be easy to perceive the different configuration of the Mother Church of Jerusalem and of the later one of Antioch in Syria (as well as of the other churches developed from it). It will be convenient to examine this information in more detail[16].

gospel, accessible only to them, which had come *through a secret transmission made by the Apostles*, or that even exceeded the degree of evangelical consciousness the Apostles had at that moment. Irenaeus then takes the first case and argues thus: let us examine those churches we know were founded by one of the Apostles and from that moment have preserved an uninterrupted succession, to see if they affirm something of what the heretics are saying. And he argues: «The tradition of the Apostles is clear for anyone and can be seen by all who wish to know the truth. In effect: we are in a position to reckon up those who were by the apostles instituted bishops in their succession up to our own times; and these never taught anything similar to these delusions [of the heretics]. If the apostles had known «hidden mysteries», which they were in the habit of imparting secretly to the «perfect ones», they would have imparted them, before anyone, to those to whom they were also committing the Churches themselves. For they were desirous that these men should be very «perfect» and above reproach (cf. 1 Tm 3:2) in all things, since they were leaving them behind as their successors to hold their same role as teachers» (III, 3,1).

And a little later he continues: «Suppose a dispute arises even if it is about something not very important, should we not have recourse to the most ancient Churches with which the apostles held constant interaction, and learn from them what is certain and clear in regard to the present question?» (III, 4, 1). Here it is not even the formal authority of those Churches that is being claimed, but rather *the material possibility that those Churches had retained more exactly the teaching of the Apostles* by their privileged conditions. Furthermore, Irenaeus assumes that there was a time when the Apostles had their teachings written down because «such was the horror which the apostles and their disciples had against holding even verbal communication with any corrupters of the truth» (Book III, 3, 4). With that, as it were, the purely material apostolicity and the formal apostolicity were sufficiently and inseparably united. So, henceforth, an appeal to apostolic authority must *also* include an appeal to the content of that authority. And that moment is characterized by the writings in the New Testament, and more concretely by the gospels: all of them (as Irenaeus seems to believe) refer in an unbroken line to an Apostle and they present the testimony of Jesus. But even so —he continues— a complete synthesis of both types of apostolicity can only be found if all *four gospels are taken together*. And if one of the gospels is taken in isolation without the others, the continuity with the Apostles can again be broken notwithstanding the formality of the succession. This —affirms Irenaeus— is what the Ebionites do with Matthew's gospel, the Marcionites with Luke's, some Gnostics with Mark's, and the Valentinians with John's (Cf. III, 11, 17).

A similar conclusion would be found in the analysis of another classic text: that of Tertullian's *De praescriptione haereticorum*, No. 32, with his famous cry «edant ergo origins ecclesiarum suarum...!», etc.

16 Cf. ROLOFF J., *Hechos de los Apóstoles*. Madrid: Cristiandad, 1984. RIUS J., *El camino de Pablo a la misión de los paganos. Comentario exegético a Hechos 13-28*. Madrid: Cristiandad, 1984.

According to some historians, the first Christian church of Jerusalem stopped going to the Temple *expiatory* cult, even though they still went there to pray. But instead it gradually started to organize itself in *a very similar way to the «presbyteral councils» of Old Testament Judaism*. The first point shows that they had a very clear comprehension of the expiatory meaning —new and definitive— of Jesus' Death and Resurrection. While in relation to the second point there is no sacrosanct or binding information that can link it to Jesus Christ himself or his words. Not even the very important fact of the presence of the Apostles in that community.

In fact the Lucan view presented in *Acts* makes it possible to trace, more or less, the following evolution:

a) «Apostles». At the beginning the group is bound together by the «teachings of the Apostles» (2:42), which later on is characterized as «to bear witness to the Resurrection of the Lord Jesus» (4:33). When the first problem within the community arises, the Apostles are the ones who «call together the whole community of the disciples» (6:2), but it is the *whole community which approves* the proposal of the Apostles (6:5). When the Judaeo-Hellenists are forced to flee by the persecution, they take their own missionary initiatives, without any assignment from the Apostles, to the point that, when the Apostles perceive the success of the particular initiative of the deacon Philip in that region, they decide to send no less than Peter and John to Samaria (cf.8:5ff)[17]. When Peter has the first intuition and initial experience about the mission among the Gentiles, there is a part of the community (of the «Apostles and brothers») which confronted him (cf. 11:1-3). Until this moment one can perceive an Apostles-community interaction, with a clear and logical role of responsibility on the part of the Apostles. But it is a leadership of searching, more than the implementation of formulas. Maybe because of this it always seems to request the approval of the whole community —naturally something which is easier in not too big communities by the very nature of things.

Chapter 2

57

---

17 Everything seems to indicate that Acts 8:5ff does not refer to the Apostle Philip but to the deacon of the same name, about whom 6:5 speaks, as the first preaching in Samaria took place during the flight from Jerusalem, when «those who had been scattered went about preaching the word» (8:4). This seems to be confirmed in Acts 21:8 where Philip «the evangelist» appears and it is made clear that he «was one of the Seven». Cf. BOLOFF J., *Hechos de los Apóstoles*. Madrid: Cristiandad, 1984, 183-184.

b) «Elders». Nonetheless, a bit later, when in Antioch they decide to have a collection in favor of the brothers in Jerusalem, the proceeds will be sent to «the elders» there (11:30). It is worth noting that here there is no mention of the Apostles, even though these could have been included in the term (more encompassing in itself), or could have been expressly left aside because it was an «administrative» measure not corresponding to what Acts 6:1ff had mentioned as «right for» the Apostles.

c) «Apostles and elders». The fact is that from here on, when *Acts* refers to the «leadership» of the first church of Jerusalem, it will designate it as «the Apostles and *elders*»[18]. This terminology now seems constant whenever the church of Jerusalem has to make a decision. One gets the impression that —in spite of the «natural» and indisputable authority of the Apostles— the first church has assumed the configuration typical of the Old Testament tradition. In fact, a few chapters before we had encountered «elders» in speaking about the ones responsible in the *Jewish* community of Jerusalem for persecuting the infant Church (cf. Acts 4:5.8.23; 6:12). The assumption has been made in a natural way, without traumas and without questioning the natural authority of the Apostles, either[19]. But it is remarkable that the author of *Acts* has no problem designating the leaders of the *Jewish* community in Jerusalem as «*priests* and elders» (cf.23:14; 24:1;4.23:;25:15), something he *carefully takes care* not to say of Christians. This confirms what we have said in the first part.

3.2. NOR IS THERE A PREVIOUS MODEL FOR RESOLVING NEW SITUATIONS OF SITUATIONS OF CONFLICT

Soon after the beginning of the life of the infant Church, a peaceful separation took place in Jerusalem (without the breaking of communion or contact) between the first Palestinian Christians and the Greek-speaking Jewish Christians. This separation seemed at the beginning to be a pacific and harmonious coexistence of both communities. Later on, for *external* reasons —such as the persecution against the Judaeo-Hellenists— it derived into the establishment of another ecclesial community in Antioch of Syria. From this other community, much more alive and creative than the one in Jerusalem, there seems to have

---

18 Cf. 15:2; 4,22;16:4; and it must be noted how «elders» reappear in chapter 18, the moment Jerusalem starts appearing again.

19 In this natural authority there are also tensions between the line of the respected James «brother of the Lord» and the more universal line of Peter, with a clear advantage for the latter.

come about not only the cutting of the umbilical cord that still united the believers in Jesus to Judaism («it was in Antioch that the disciples were first called Christians» Acts 11:26) but almost all the mission and theology of the primitive Church.

Paul, who felt more uncomfortable in Jerusalem, seems to be incorporated into that church in Antioch, sent from there on different missionary journeys[20]. But this community always maintained communication with the church of Jerusalem, notwithstanding the conflicting circumstances in which they found themselves and in spite of the fact that when the Hellenist Jews departed from Jerusalem the Palestinian community seems to have moved to a more conservative position.

That is how, in substance, according to the majority of exegetes, one should understand the episode of the «creation of deacons» in Acts 6:1ff. It is true that if we stick to the first meaning of the text of *Acts*, maybe we should say simply that the first Church *created new ministries as new situations began to appear* or as need demanded. And this lesson would be enough for the object of our study. But it is also true that the exegetes tend today to give a version of this episode which goes further than the *literal* meaning of the text of *Acts*: not only were new ministries created[21], but another different *community*, for we see immediately that these who should be simple «deacons» devote themselves to the ministry *of the word* which the Apostles seemed to have reserved for themselves when they instituted the Seven (cf. Acts 6:4 with 6:8ff). Perhaps Stephen even proved himself to be much more provocative in the presence of the Sanhedrin than the Apostles had hitherto shown themselves to be (or simply he had a much more radical theology than they did) and brought down upon the Judaeo-Hellenistic Church the full weight of persecution[22].

---

20 The facts about Paul in Acts 9-15 do not seem to harmonize easily with what the same Apostle says about himself in Gal 1-2. For historical questions see again Roloff's book, even though one should note that the author of the Prologue to that book considers as one of the most unacceptable points «the association —or disassociation— of Paul with his community in Antioch» (15 and 316ff). For Paul's biographical data one can see the second part of VIDAL S. *Iniciación a Pablo*, Santander: Sal Terrae, 2008. And by the same author: *De Tarso a Roma*, Santander: Sal Terrae, 2007.

21 In reality the text of Acts 6:1ff does not speak at all about «deacons» expect for the general use of the word «service» that holds equally for the daily distribution (6:2) as for the preaching of the Apostles (6:5).

22 See on this subject the excellent article by AGUIRRE R., «La iglesia cristiana de Antioquía de Siria» in *RIT 10* (January-April 1987), 63-88.

Let us then say, at least, that in either of those two hypotheses the Church makes a decision, not appealing to a constitution or law given already by Jesus, but trying, *at the same time*, to respond to a historical need and not to break the communion among its members. We need no more for our objective.

3.3. DIVERSITY OF MODELS

Once the new community in Antioch was established, one has the impression that it was structured in a different way to the one in Jerusalem: in a way that, on the one hand, was much more charismatic, and on the other much more missionary. Perhaps too, at the outset, it was a smaller community, in spite of its enormous influence in the later transmission of Christianity. But the fact is that the *structure* of this new community did not seem to create problems for the «prophets» who sometimes descended on Antioch from Jerusalem (cf. Acts 11:27), while other decisions about the life of this community did.

The first reference to the structure of the community of Antioch tells us that «there were in the Church of Antioch prophets and teachers» (Acts 13:1), and it gives us also the name of many of them. From Acts 11:27 and 15:33 we must deduce that such «prophets» existed in the community of Jerusalem, too, even though the author of *Acts* never mentions them explicitly when speaking of the internal life of that community, but only when mentioning its relationship with the community of Antioch. We have no definition of the exact content of that expression, but we can come close to it from Acts 15:33, which tells us that the envoys from Jerusalem to Antioch, sent to communicate the decisions of the first «council», «who were themselves prophets, exhorted and strengthened the brothers with many words». They were, then, men with charisma, with the gift of the Word, with pedagogic abilities that testified and strengthened, whose work derived more from their charisma than from the assignment given by the community. In Antioch they probably stood for the Apostles who remained in Jerusalem, without breaking contact or communion with them. But the curious and important detail is that *never do they speak about «elders»* when referring to the Antioch community.

The second reference to the ministries of the Church of Antioch is that from among those «prophets and teachers» there seem to have emerged the first itinerant missionaries (or «charismatic missionaries» to use a recent fortunate expression). The book of *Acts* confirms this explicitly in relation to Paul and Barnabas (cf. 13:2-3). It also calmly calls these missionaries «apostles», at least when it refers to their evangelical work (cf. Acts 14:4,14). Here the consecrated word has taken on, for the community of Antioch, a different meaning to the one it had for the community in Jerusalem[23].

A third reference we find is that these missionaries «after they had proclaimed the good news to a city and made a considerable number of disciples», when they said goodbye «they appointed elders for them in each church, with prayer and fasting commended them to the Lord» (Acts 14:23). Another trace of this same information we find further on when Paul wants to arrive sooner at Jerusalem and decides not to go through Ephesus. He nonetheless calls the «elders» of that church to say goodbye to them (Acts 20:17). In the somewhat dramatic speech he delivers, Paul calls these men *«episkopus»* (20:28), which shows the indistinctiveness between both words, as we will see. It does not matter if what is reflected here is the Pauline concept of ministry or that of the author of *Acts*. What is important is that the first mission of the Greek Jews had copied the structure of the church of Jerusalem, even if this is due more to an actual need than to the obligation of copying the model of that church[24]. At this time there was no problem in the fact that those elders were recent converts: what else could they be? But later on when the churches were more established, it will become problematic to elect as presbyter a new convert and at the same time inexperienced (cf. 1 Tim 3:6).

This fact is important, too, because here we have an important reference to the laying on of hands. In reality it is an Old Testament rite (cf. Deut 34:9), as was also the baptismal rite. But now it will receive a new meaning, related to the gift of the Spirit, a fundamental fact for the early church: so fundamental that its importance and the frequent references to this gift contrast greatly to the little or no importance that the Spirit seems to have in the official life of the Church today.

23 See ROLOFF J., *Hechos de los Apóstoles* (Madrid: Cristianidad, 1984), 62ff. for the four meanings of the word «apostle»: a) the Twelve, b) the «witnesses to the Resurrection», c) the witnesses to both the Resurrection and the earthly life of Jesus (this appears to be Luke's own concept, though it would exclude none other than Paul), and d) the meaning in the Church of Antioch. This certain «ambiguity» could play a role in defining the notion of formal apostolicity.
24 Even though we are now trying to present what Luke describes and not the historical reality, it could be convenient to point out that more than one exegete considers that the observation in Acts 14:23 is tinged with the idealization sometimes provided by Luke. There is other information which shows that not all of the Pauline mission cities had elders. (Cf. BROWN R., *Las Iglesias que los Apóstoles nos dejaron*, Desclée de Brouwer, Bilbao 1986, 33).

In spite of it, at this stage in the life of the first church, the meaning of the connection between the laying on of hands and the Spirit is still very broad and vague. Even in *Acts* we find this same rite of the laying on of hands with a meaning that is not the one we are here commenting on, but a sort of «accompaniment» which distinguishes the baptism of John from that of Jesus (cf. Acts 8.17;19:4-6; see also 28:8). It is not clear either, in those first uses, if it is a *communication* of the Spirit (as is suggested in Acts 6:6) or if it is the *acknowledgment* of a gift of the Spirit already communicated (which is what it seems to be in Acts 13:3)[25]. The New Testament retains both meanings; maybe it is only later, with the need to name the Apostles' successors, that it moved toward the first meaning, thus leading to the later vision of ordination as a «source» of powers, etc. See what we shall say when we speak about the «Pastoral Epistles».

Finally, there is a last reference which does not necessarily contradict the previous one but complements it. On occasions, when facing different decisions taken by some of these communities (in Thessalonica and Beroea), there is no mention of elders or of prophets, but only of «the brothers»[26]. This is a much broader term than that used to designate the whole community[27]. Now it will be *the brothers* who will decide to make Paul and Silas leave Beroea, or Paul go alone to Athens, at times of conflict in their preaching (cf 17:10.14). It is not the affected disciples who take this decision, maybe because the members of those communities recognize that they know the ground better and feel responsible for the life of these apostles. And if the decision-making body of these communities is mentioned with such an encompassing term («the brothers»), it can also be due to the reduced and incipient character of those groups. But it reflects equally that there was no previous model for structuring those groups.

3.4. COMMUNITY IN PLURALITY

The life of those two communities develops then within a *communion in diversity.* We do not even know up to what point the Apostles were involved in all the expansion and growth of the church of Antioch. It seems rather that the facts imposed themselves upon them.

25 Later on the Church will still be obliged sometimes to distinguish between a *cheirotonía* (or imposition of hands in the sense of transmission of powers) and a mere *cheirothesía* (simple installation of an office). See the third part of this work.

26 In the second part of *Acts*, when speaking of the later trips of Paul, the expression used is «the disciples» (for example, 21:4,16). Maybe this designation is used when Christians are not known, since when reaching Jerusalem again the phrase used is «the brothers and sisters» (21:17).

27 See, for example, Acts 9:30; 11:1,29;14:2;15:1...

On the other hand, we always find in Antioch a clear concern for communion with the church of Jerusalem. And it is a communion which tries to be achieved *through the search for consensus on the minimum and respect on all other aspects*, more than by imposing on others their own way. When the first conflicts arise, the people of Antioch immediately decide to «go to Jerusalem» to see the «Apostles and elders» (cf. Acts 15:2; an echo of this same attitude in Gal 1:17; 2:1-2).

In opposition to the creativity of the church of Antioch, the church in Jerusalem portrayed itself on several occasions by a useless endeavor to impose on all its own line of thought. It is true that there also seems to have been in Jerusalem men such as Barnabas, «full of the Holy Spirit and faith», who knew how to understand and support Antioch's initiative[28]. But the dominant mentality seems characterized by that attempt to impose on everyone their own way, assuming —because of their Jewish tradition— the right to be God's sole interpreters. I already mentioned that such an endeavor in the end had to give way. And in this softening the «Apostles and elders» in the community of Jerusalem seem to have had a wise and decisive role. The so-called «Council of Jerusalem» (Acts 15) suggests an important way of exercising the ecclesial ministry in these three points:

a) The assembly bans certain jealous and intolerant behavior which has «disturbed unnecessarily» the faithful (cf. 15:10 and clearer still 15:24-28). They make it clear, too, that those behaving like that «went out from us without our authorization» (15:24).

b) They strive to have a resolution adopted not only by Peter or James but by the whole assembly of «Apostles and elders» (cf. 15:23).

c) In spite of all this or precisely because of it, the adopted solution is something of a «compromise»: the open line of Peter prevails, but the final document, even though it speaks of «burdening only with what is fundamental», imposes things that in reality were not indispensable (cf. 15:28,29)[29]. James in turn probably compromised on the subject of circumcision in exchange for saving that series of practices in relation to the flesh of animals offered as

---

28 Cf. Acts 11:19-24, even though this passage does not fit too well with the following v.25.

29 At least according to the presentation of *Acts*, which maybe mixes the conclusions of the post-council with those of the council, as Paul in Gal 2 does not present things in this way, and he seems more trustworthy since Luke does not appear to have participated in the council and he tends to follow the «irenic» path in ecclesial conflicts.

sacrifices to the idols and the prohibition of blood, etc. And James sustains his position strongly about these practices because he thinks that otherwise the reading of Moses that continues to be done on Saturdays in the meetings of the converted Jews becomes useless and ridiculous (cf. 15:21). At that moment and from his localized perspective James could see nothing else. But it is doubtful that —if those precepts were really from the council— Paul did pay much attention to them in his later preaching[30]. James, instead, saved for all the communities the prohibition of incestuous relationships to which seems to refer the controversial word *porneia*[31]. And only the passing of time was able to clear up these different points which were taken as being of the same magnitude. This lesson has been confirmed by history many, many times and just as many times forgotten, either due to the impatience of some or to the reactionary stubbornness of others.

3.5. CONCLUSION

The decisions taken by the Church of Acts *were suggested or imposed by the most communitarian discernment possible of historical situations and did not spring from the application of a program previously drawn up by Jesus.* Moreover it is legitimate to affirm, with a certain provocative wording, that the history of the early Church did not exactly know either an episcopacy or papacy, but a creative variety in communion —not always easy— with the Apostolate. In it is shown that ecclesial ministry is not configured in the same way at a time of mission or in a missionary situation as at a time of structuring and conservatism of the mission already achieved[32]. And, according to *Acts*, one should add that the unity of the early Church did not take place through uniformity in ministerial forms and ecclesial structure, but more by reference to what Jesus represented and concern for the poor, as is shown in Acts 11:29-30 and in the so-called «testament of Paul» in 20:35 (information confirmed by Paul himself in Gal 2:10).

---

30   Acts 16:4 does not seem to harmonize with 1Cor 8:8ff and Rom 14:2-17.

31   Cf. Lev 18; cf. Also AGUIRRE R., «La iglesia cristiana de Antioquía de Siria» en *RLT 10* (enero-abril 1987) 77. If the *porneia* of Acts 15:29 refers to the same conduct as 1Cor 5:1, we can add that Paul (who does not seem to have kept in excess the precepts about food) was on the other hand very strict in the application of this other matter.

32   Deliberately I do not want to call such structuring and conservative activity of what has been achieved «pastoral» (as is done, for example, in the so-called «Pastoral Epistles»), because today, at a time of such profound historical change, the «pastoral» care of the un-converted or Christians «from birth» is practically a *missionary* work and not merely a conservative one. In this sense I believe it is right to speak of a «second evangelization». I refer to this work's conclusion (4,1).

We will reach a similar conclusion, although enriched, through the study of other testimonies in the New Testament.

4

Plurality of charismatic ministries in the Pauline Churches

The communities addressed by the letters of the so-called «*corpus paulinum*» (we will not consider here the «Pastoral» ones) permit us to suspect the existence of a *different type of ecclesial ministry and organization* from what we have found in *Acts*.

To start with, in those writings the presbyteral structure is not reflected at all and the word «*presbyteros*» does not appear even once (the same could be said in relation to the community in Antioch of Syria). Nonetheless, several references and explicit allusions indicate there existed a broad range of ministries, mostly of charismatic origin, in those Pauline communities. And that Paul believed that, behind the diversity of functions, can be found the unifying mission of the Spirit, one and the same for all.

Almost the entire reflection can be focused on two classical passages: one from the *First Letter to the Corinthians* and the other from *Ephesians*[33]. Although it will be convenient to complete the first with another quick reference from the *Letter to the Romans* and gather them together in the context of an important reflection of Paul about the community.

4.1. MINISTRIES AND CORPORAL FUNCTIONS

The famous image of the Church as «Body» presented itself to Paul precisely as an explanation of the variety in the ecclesial ministry. The principle stated by Paul in Rom 12:6 is that, just as in a body there are diverse functions, all of them unified by the same vital principle, so also in the Church there are various

---

[33] The Pauline link of *Ephesians* is much questioned today by exegetes and, at least, it can be stated that its ecclesiology is very different to that of 1 *Corinthians*. While the latter possesses an ecclesiology of the *local* community, in *Ephesians* we find a highly elaborated theological vision of the *universal* Church: she is the immaculate Spouse of the Lord, the Body of Christ or Sacrament of the Summation of all in Him, the fullness of the total-Christ, which comes to himself as reality becomes unto Christ (cf. 1:20-23). Nothing of this appears in 1 Corinthians. Nonetheless, and for what is of interest now, it is legitimate to leave aside this difference and underline the point both have in common: a *diversity* of charismatic ministries in the *unity* of the Spirit, whether speaking of the local church or of the universal Church.

«charismas according to different gifts». And when immediately Paul enumerates those gifts, we realize it is about real ecclesial functions.

The list of ministries we find in Rom 12 (not pretending to be complete or systematic, just exemplary) is the following: *prophecy, service, teaching (didaskalia), exhortation, distribution and leading* (cf. Rom 12:6-8). It is almost impossible to pin down the exact function of each of these «gifts» and what differentiates them. But one suspects that some determine functions in relation to the word (prophecy, teaching and exhortation or consolation), others seem to be more «administrative» (service or «diakonia» and giving or distribution), and another seems to have a more decisive or authoritative character. It is curious, though, that this final one (leading, «presidency») occupies almost the last place in the list. In any case, what is really important is that behind them lies «love that is sincere» (Rom 12:9).

So, what we encounter here in this quick glance we will find again, much more structured, in 1 Cor 12, also referring to the image of the body, but underlining more specifically that it is the *one same Spirit* who gives life to that Body (cf. 1 Cor 12:4,7,8,9,11). Let us see this.

4.2. DIVERSITY OF FUNCTIONS AND UNITY OF THE VITAL PRINCIPLE

In this chapter Paul has a double list (vv. 8ff and 28ff). The first is terribly vague and difficult to classify. Observing the order of the text we seem to find:

a) gifts of the word (message of wisdom, of knowledge, of faith: 8-9);

b) gifts of healing (9b) and miracles (10); and

c) a third group which again mentions functions connected to the word, but, perhaps one should say an «authorized» word: speaking *in the name* of God, *discernment* of spirits, speaking in different tongues or the *interpretation* of tongues (10).

It is not clear if we can establish a parallel between this list and the one in *Romans*. But it is not of great import, because what is decisive at this moment in the Pauline letter is not the content of the list, but the two phrases that frame it, in the manner of a biblical «inclusion», which we must highlight.

At the beginning of the paragraph: Using a phrase of probable Trinitarian origin, Paul repeats:

a) Different charisma, but only one Spirit.

b) Different services, but only one Lord.

c) Different functions, but only one God (1 Cor 12:4-6).

The parallelism of the phrase permits us to deduce the identity between charisma, service and function. They are different forms of designating the ecclesial ministry.

At the end of the paragraph: All these are the work of *one and the same* Spirit, who distributes them to each person just as he determines (1Cor 12:11).

In short: *unity* of the *different,* just as in the human body (cf. 12-26). An ecclesiology which has not committed the sin of extinguishing pneumatology (cf. 1 Thess 4:19) will always be an ccclesiology of *communion in plurality, which* belongs to the essence itself of the Church. Its falsification will be a juridical uniformity which will nullify differences and unify only what is undifferentiated. But this constitutes a serious ecclesiological deformation more useful for describing any human «ghetto» than Christ's Church. The image of a dead machine would, in this case, be more apt than that of a living body.

This text does not end here. Happily for us, Paul returns to the subject (12:28-31) and now he presents a more technical list of ecclesial ministries, as he introduces his list with the words: «God has placed in his Church…», and immediately comes the following list (which even seems to be made with the intention of establishing a hierarchy, as is shown by the adverbs):

«first of all apostles,
second prophets,
third teachers,
then miracles,
then gifts of healing, of helping,
of guidance, and of different kinds of tongues» (12:28-29).

With certain «fear and trembling» maybe we can see here, again, a classification of ministries «of the word», ministries «of assistance» (miracles, healings, etc.) and ministries «of authority». We would have in this way a scheme almost identical to that of *Romans.* Even with the coincidence that here, too, the leadership functions are practically at the end of the list, even though the word employed here *(kuberneseis)* is not the same as in *Romans (proistamenos),* which seems a more consecrated and classical term. This could have a natural explanation in that small communities have less need of authoritarian decisions. But it still stands out, not just because Paul himself has introduced into his list those hierarchical adverbs (first, second…), but most of all by the juxtaposition of «guidance» with «different kinds of tongues» which, we already know, was a charism with little importance for Paul (cf. 1Cor 14).

Again, as in *Romans*, the list closes with an inovacation (in this case much longer) of what is the real structuring work of the Church: love (cf. chapter 13). Without love whatever ministry or charism has no value: not prophecy or knowledge (13:2a), nor performing miracles (13:2b), nor the most excellent caring tasks (13:3). The references of these phrases to the list in chapter 12 seem more than probable.

4.3. THE SURVIVAL OF THIS DOCTRINE IN THE *LETTER TO THE EPHESIANS*

We find similar teaching in the *Letter to the Ephesians*, even though the ecclesiological horizon of this work —as we have already mentioned— seems to refer more to the universal Church.

To begin with, the structuring principle of the Church is the same as in *Romans* and 1Cor: «there is one body and one Spirit» (4:4). The unifying elements are not, then, merely the structural or ministerial ones, but the «Spiritual» ones: the same Lord, the same faith, the same baptism, the same God and Father (4:5-6). And this unity is displayed immediately because «to each one of us grace has been given as Christ apportioned it» (Eph 4:7; cf. with 1Cor 12:11). Then we find another list of ministries: «So Christ himself gave the apostles, the prophets, the evangelists, the pastors and teachers» (4:11). But the object of this variety is the construction of the body of Christ, until we all reach unity in the faith, the whole measure of the fullness of Christ (cf. 4:12-13).

A circle is thus closed that goes from the unity to unity, through the enrichment of plurality. A circle that appears as very much loved in the New Testament.

The scheme of unity in plurality is the same one as before. The list coincides with *1 Corinthians* in the priority it gives to «Apostles and prophets» and maybe also in the fact that the ministry of authority is not placed in the first place, either, even though now it appears linked with «teacher». On the other hand, we do not find here those ministries we have called «administrative» or «of assistance». But probably one should say again that this list does not pretend to be an «organization chart» of the structure of the Church, but rather a literary example of the fact that *the variety of ministries is a gift of the one Lord*. The uniformity or concentration of power would be, for Pauline theology, a form of «idolatry» since it would pretend to reproduce, at the level of what is created and limited, the Transcendental simplicity of God.

Up to now we have been dealing with the facts of the Pauline Churches. We now offer a dual reflection, not about the theology at the root of these facts, but about the lists of ministries that we have found.

a) In the first place, we have suggested the possibility that, even though none of these lists constitutes a technical classification, they are near enough, not so much in the *concrete* functions listed as in the «chapters» or groups of functions mentioned. In a first general approximation I have spoken about the «ministries of the word, of assistance and of authority». Examining this rough classification in a bit more detail, it could be useful to recall a famous reflection of Ernst Bloch, made popular in the past by Álvarez Bolado.

According to Bloch, any community on the way needs four indispensable services: it needs leaders, teachers, doctors and singers or poets. For Bloch, this classification comes from the nature itself of what constitutes a developing community or a people on the march. In an indispensable way it needs teaching (or the ideology that enlightens the goals and minds); absolutely essential is a leadership which opens up the path; finally, it also needs solidarity and assistance: both material help (represented in Bloch by medical doctors and in Paul by alms, healing, etc.) and spiritual help (what Paul calls «exhortation» or work of comfort and discernment of spirits and Bloch in a vaguer way typifies as «poets» and singers[34]). These are the tasks of the ecclesial ministry, whether they remain divided or assembled.

I have carried out this approach to show that ministries arise in the Church *from the nature itself of things* and from the very needs of the people of God, not from a sort of legal action or founding document written by Jesus Christ or one of the Apostles. This does not preclude, evidently, that the people of God be *all* referenced to Jesus, with whom it connects through the group of the Twelve, who were around Jesus and «around» the early Church.

b) Secondly, and bearing in mind our present ecclesiastical context, it can seem striking that none of those lists mention «bishops-presbyters-deacons»[35].

---

34 I cannot resist mentioning the beautiful song by Horacio Guarany, made popular by Mercedes Sosa: «If the singer is silenced, life is silenced…».

35 With the exception of the greetings in *Philippians* (1:1), where Paul expressly mentions, alongside the community, their «bishops and deacons», an expression used with the same meaning which we will see later in the «Pastoral Letters» and which must be due to some historical fact, because all the other occasions when he greets or says goodbye, Paul speaks generically of «the saints», «the brothers» or «the Church». In any case, if he wishes to mention people who play a concrete role he normally speaks of «collaborators» or «those who work».

On the other hand, perhaps one should say that the functions which appear so diversified in the Pauline *corpus* will again be found in other pages of the New Testament, but concentrated and assigned always in a general way to the group of «presbyters». So they will talk of presbyters in relation to the task of teaching (c.f. Titus 1:5-9), in praying for the sick (Jas 5:14), when speaking of the elders (1Tim 5:17; 1Pet 5:2)... Here we are perhaps seeing a first takeover of functions, just as we shall see later.

What is the reason for this development? Probably, the charismatic makeup of the Pauline churches could not be sustained once the great authority of the Apostle disappeared and the size and interrelation of the churches had grown. This evolution thus should not be seen as purely negative. But, in spite of everything, the charismatic eagerness of the Pauline churches should have been more present in the Church, at least as an aspiration from which it is impossible to break completely, as a sort of beacon towards which the Church should be oriented, even if in the end it still remains very far from it. That charismatic eagerness comes supported by a (brief) theology of the community, enormously Christian, which Paul himself presented in one of his first letters (1 Thess 5:12-22). This last point is the one left for examination before we conclude the present section.

4.5. THE PAULINE THEOLOGY OF COMMUNITY

«*Now we ask you, brothers and sisters, to acknowledge those who work hard among you, who care for you in the Lord and who admonish you. Hold them in the highest regard in love because of their work. Live in peace with each other. And we urge you, brothers and sisters, warn those who are idle and disruptive, encourage the disheartened, help the weak, be patient with everyone. Make sure that nobody pays back wrong for wrong, but always strive to do what is good for each other and for everyone else. Rejoice always, pray continually, give thanks in all circumstances; for this is God's will for you in Christ Jesus. Do not quench the Spirit. Do not treat prophecies with contempt but test them all; hold on to what is good, reject every kind of evil*» (1Thess 5:12-22).

Let us observe briefly the characteristics listed in this paragraph:
a) Recognition of the work of the leaders (vv. 12-13): it is hard work and rarely well-recognized; but it is an acknowledgement that implies that the leaders

are «among you» and not «over» you because, in the latter case, recognition would be misrepresented as adulation.

b) Special attention to minors (v. 14).

c) Change of values in relationships (v. 15): do not pay back wrong for wrong, but strive to do good to all.

d) Happiness that comes from faith and the experience of receiving freely (vv. 16-18).

e) Liberty that does not stifle (v. 19): because by stifling a person the Spirit itself can be killed, as so many times will happen to the later Church.

f) Capacity for discernment (vv. 20-21).

A tremendous community program! In my opinion one can say that here we have a true Magna Carta for the Christian community. And any community, any «church» should constantly compare itself against this program.

Would it be exaggerated to think that precisely from this Pauline vision of the community has emerged the later structuring of the ministries in the Pauline churches? This would explain the persuasive capacity these churches have today for many Christians, as well as the need for the «official» Church to look toward them with courage and to let itself be challenged by them[36].

And maybe one should add that such persuasive capacity has its price reflected in the great harshness of Paul's life (prophesied in his initial experience, according to Acts 9:16). Rejected as traitor by the converted Jerusalemites (who will even try to kill him) and looked upon with suspicion by many Judaeo-Hellenists because he had persecuted them to death and they did not trust him. It is the fate of all who are not particularistic[37].

---

[36] One should remember, nonetheless, that behind these charismatic churches lay the authority of Paul, who must have been a passionate man with an authoritarian temperament which can be seen many times in his eagerness to control himself. It would be interesting to analyze in more depth his conduct in some cases where he intervened, such as the incestuous person in Corinth, or the discussion about women, in which he seems to contradict his own arguments («but in Christ it is not so…»), ending by going back on his initial inflexibility and reducing it to a «custom». See what will be said at the conclusion of this work about the spirituality of the ministry in 2Cor and the way Paul conceives or wishes to exercise his authority.

[37] See Acts 9:26.29; 21:21ff; 22:18; 26:21.

Unification of ministries and the greater structural rigidity in the «Pastoral Epistles»

Today it is almost universally accepted that the «Pastoral Epistles» were not written by Paul, even though the «St. Jerome Biblical Commentary» with weighty arguments defends the authorship by Paul of these letters.

The question is not theologically unimportant. If the «Pastorals» were by Paul, this would mean that the Apostle had ended up entering into a scheme of ecclesiastical structuring and a conception of the ministry much more centralized and authoritarian, as were the later ones which have been at the basis of the catholic concept. On the other hand, if the «Pastorals» were by Paul, they would have been written before the year 67, and so they would reflect a relatively ancient conception of the ministry and not a much later evolution (around the year 100), which has usually been affirmed. Undoubtedly both would be comfortable for the theologian.

But a systematic theologian should not enter too easily in exegetically questioned issues, and on other occasions I have already supported the idea that, in such cases, it is preferable to adopt minimalist positions with caution. Here, too, I will rely on a subjective impression, a sort of personal «linguistic feeling» that I would formulate more or less like this: if we read the «Pastorals» in Greek just after the Pauline letters, and then we were assured that the «Pastorals» were from Paul's pen, we would have a similar sensation to that of someone who read one after the other a page from García Márquez and another from Miguel Delibes and afterwards was assured that both were by the same author... At least sometimes the style says something about the person.

Of course impressions like this do not constitute an argument. They must be subjected to a more detailed analysis, as is done by New Testament specialists. But they can be another reason to add to what seems to be the general opinion of exegetes. According to this, we can suppose that the «Pastoral Epistles» first appeared possibly in Rome, at the end of the 1st century, as the work of a disciple or someone who appeals to the authority of Paul[38]. They reflect, then, an evolu-

---

38 It seems that Rome was evangelized by Christians influenced more by Jerusalem than by Antioch or Paul. This would explain Paul's interest in making contact with them, and also the excellence of that church in relation to the care of the poor (reflecting a mentality like the *Letter of James*, etc.).

tion or, at least, another way of structuring the ministry. We should comment in detail on these three features:

a) The close link between ecclesial ministry and doctrinal vigilance.
b) The information they offer about the organization of the ministry of those churches (presbyters —identified with bishops— and deacons).
c) The insistence on formal apostolicity, with the imposition of hands, as the basis of ecclesial ministry.

It is perhaps worthwhile to say a word about each of these points.

5.1.   THE NOTION OF HETERODOXY

The «Pastoral Epistles», especially the letters to Timothy, are full of long paragraphs against the sowers of false doctrines or controversial speculation[39]. Moreover, they see the appearance of these doctrines almost as a calamity announcing the end of time. And they are letters that repeat ad nauseam expressions like «sound doctrine» (1 Tim 1:10; 2 Tim 4:3; Titus 1:9); «godly teaching» (1 Tim 6:3; 2 Tim 1:13); «good deposit» (*paratheké*: 1 Tim 6:20; 2 Tim 1:14) or «trustworthy saying» (cf. 1 Tim 1:15; 2 Tim 2:11-13; Titus 3:8)... Opposing these, all the other doctrines are considered as «myths» (1 Tim 1:4-6; 6:4-20; 2 Tim 2:14,16,23)... It almost seems as if the only task of the «presbyter» is to preserve this doctrinal deposit from pollution or contamination by myths. So the ministers of the Church never appear linked to the Eucharist or Baptism.

This sort of obsession reveals perhaps not only the presence of a troubled author but of a troublesome situation: the strong crisis of identity of a still young Church which faces Gnosticism and the intent to return to a Jewish way. This anxious situation generates sometimes authoritarian flashes in the author, as if the truth were something that could be preserved by force. And this in spite of the fact that the author establishes at different moments the principle that orthodoxy can only be affirmed with magnanimity, with patience, without quarrels, etc. (cf. 2 Tim 2:24,25; 4:2). A principle usually forgotten but which also appears in the «Pastoral Epistles».

It is understandable that these meanings perturb or disgust a modern mentality obsessed by hermeneutics and by the necessary relativity and particularity of all language and, also, fiercely influenced by history in relation to the sinful tendency of the human being to confuse its own security with divine truth.

---

39 Cf. 1 Tim 1:3-10; 4:1-10, 6:3-6; 2 Tim 2:16-17; 3:19...

I sincerely believe that these worries of the modern mentality are, in principle, very legitimate. Hermeneutics is absolutely necessary (even if risky) if truth is in effect «catholic» (universal). The best way of «corrupting the deposit of faith» is not by trying to reformulate it but by trying to keep it untouched, without change, because in this case it will end fermenting or wilting. History has taught the Church this on more than one occasion. The deposit of faith can only be preserved just as living beings: by renovation.

But I think that, in spite of everything, our legitimate hermeneutical obsession does not completely justify the confusion or arguments mentioned in relation to the «Pastoral Epistles». What's more: I am afraid it is a confusion which stems from lack of hermeneutics. This is why perhaps we should make a small digression to point out that it is not legitimate to project our hermeneutical concerns on the «Pastoral Epistles», either to undermine the former or lose confidence in the latter.

The «Pastoral Epistles» are not about hermeneutical problems. For the author the orthodox doctrine is differentiated from the heterodox one by *the practices it generates* or from which it springs[40]. His worry is not merely theoretical or of understanding, but *praxis*. In reality, what is expressed in those ways of talking are ways of living: «they claim to know God but *with their actions* they deny Him» (Titus 1:16). And this we normally forget when reading them, even though the author has said it very clearly from the beginning: *the point of the doctrine is «the love that comes from a pure heart»* (1 Tim 1:5), since what the doctrine does is «to do God's work by faith» (1:4).

Now, these non-Christian practices can fit into two chapters we could formulate thus: a doctrine that is born to justify following our own selfish desires and a doctrine that wants to affirm the law instead of a pure heart, which is the one that generates real evangelical freedom. Let us examine this in more detail.

a) Heterodoxy as a «return to paganism».

One of the things the «Pastoral Epistles» attribute to the «heterodox» was that they think «godliness is a means of gain» (1 Tim 6:5). And this is a very serious danger as our author knows that «the love of money is root of all kinds of evil» (6:10). Religion, says the author, could be called «great gain» but in a very different sense than the material search for gain: precisely in that it fights against it and teaches to be satisfied with little (6:6).

---

40 Cf. 1 Tim 4:25; 6:5; 2 Tim 3:1-9; Titus 2:12.

To be able to focus life thus these «heterodox» affirm that «the resurrection has already taken place» (2 Tim 2:18), which will lead them to believe that their will has no opposition; but with this they will only do the devil's will (cf. 2 Tim 2:25). This is why the only thing they want is «to suit their own desires» and so they search for a great number of teachers to say what they want to hear (2 Tim 4:3)[41]. But this is precisely what had been done by the Christians when they were pagans (cf. Titus 3:3).

And this same outlook is reflected also in a long passage of 2 Pet (2:12-20), from which it will be convenient to extract at least one phrase that summarizes perfectly what is at stake here: «they promise them freedom, while they themselves are slaves of depravity —for people are slaves to whatever has mastered them» (v. 19). This phrase sums up to perfection what was at stake in the first of the doctrinal battlefields of the «Pastoral Epistles».

b) Heterodoxy as a «return to Judaism».

Opposite to those self-deluded there are others who «want to be teachers of the Law» (1 Tim 1:7; cf. Titus 2:9), but whose wisdom is reduced to prohibiting marriage and certain supposedly impure foods (1 Tim 4:3), when in reality «everything God created is good» (4:4). Equally the «foolish controversies about the law» that Titus is warned against (3:9) come from men who affirm that there are impure things and do not realize that they the impure ones: «To the pure all things are pure, but to those who are corrupted and do not believe, nothing is pure. In fact, both their minds and consciences are corrupted» (Titus 1:15).

This, then, is the heterodoxy the «Pastoral Epistles» seem to be fighting against: a pagan way of living by which the selfish desire of man is pure and a Jewish way of living by which things are not pure and the person has to purify itself with rites and abstentions. In reality, the theoretical question is *where freedom lies* (as was shown in 2 Pet 2:19): in the works of desire or in the repression of desire by the works of the Law. It is the same controversy of Paul against pagans and Jews. And the answer is neither in one nor in the other. Freedom is in the new and good heart.

In this sense I think that in the «Pastoral Epistles» there is much less novelty than is pretended: in this point they coincide with all of the New Testament. Or, in any case, the novelty will be more of *tone* (brought about by the crisis situation and the youth of the churches)[42] than of *substance*. The opposite impres-

---

41 Cf. also 1 Tim 6:9; 2 Tim 3:6; Titus 2:12…
42 Note, for example, the mention of *fear* in 1 Tim 5:20.

sion comes from projecting onto the «Pastoral Epistles» *later* problems, as are our own hermeneutical questions. Instead, if we maintain the criteria for orthodoxy found here we could wonder, for example, where the heresy was in the first dispute of Luther against indulgences…

The subsequent complexity of the problem grows, too, because throughout history more than once ecclesiastical authority has used the very notion of orthodoxy *for those things the «Pastoral Epistles» attack as radical heterodoxy*: to justify eagerness for money or living according to the personal desire for power, etc., etc. But, I repeat, these are really *later* problems.

So from all of this arises a very important conclusion: if such «orthodoxy» belongs to the mission of the ecclesial ministers recipients of these letters, then the ecclesial ministry has, before any other «power» a *task of giving example* in the truth. This means: an *evangelical* task of giving example and not merely an «ethical» one or one pertaining to the Law. It would be an example of the freedom of love. It would not be a false example of self-deceit in the interest of self-concealment or in the interest of the system, but that true example of honesty with reality that Newman called «not sinning against the light». It would be important never to forget this conclusion which should be a decisive criteria at the hour of electing or discerning the ultimate people responsible for the Church, as our Church gives today more the impression of that example in the interest of the system than of the other example of honesty with reality.

5.2.   THE COLLEGE OF «BISHOPS» OR «DEACONS»

The structure of the ministry revealed by the «Pastoral Epistles» has been determined with sufficient exactness and is also well known. So, in this section we will limit ourselves to reproducing facts that are common knowledge and can be found in any manual or commentary. The «Pastoral Epistles» give an indication of the existence of *two groups of leaders* in each church. The members of the first group are called, indistinctly, «bishops» (*episkopoi*) or «elders»; the second, «deacons». The *Nueva Biblia Española*, with a very valid intuition, translates them as «those responsible» and «the assistants» respectively. Let us say a word about each.

a) In relation to the first group, *the identity between the office of bishop and the one of elder is a fact established not only for those letters, but for the rest of the documents of the New Testament* where this terminology appears. It is about two words, one of Greek origin and the other perhaps of Jewish Jerusalem origin; and here we have a first glimpse of their merger.

When the author writes to Timothy that «whoever desires to be an overseer desires a noble task» (1 Tim 3:1ff), he is not blessing many secret aspirations to a mitre, but he is merely stating that it is a good thing to wish to enter in the group of those who concern themselves with the community. When, a little later, he again speaks of the leading group he calls them «elders» (cf. 5:17) and this ambivalence is confirmed by several other passages in the New Testament. In the same «Pastoral Epistles» we again find some very similar instructions (Titus 1:5ff) and there those who almost immediately receive the name of «bishops» (v. 7) are called «elders» (v. 5). But even outside the «Pastoral Epistles», in the narrative of *Acts* (20:17ff), Paul talks to the leading group of the city of Ephesus calling them «bishops» (20:28) when some time before he had mentioned them as «elders» (20:17). And in the *corpus paulinum*, the heading of the *Letter to the Philippians* greets the «bishops and deacons» of that church (Phil 1:1). The fact that he does not mention the elders could not be explained if they were not equal to the bishops.

The work of this first group seems to be dual: to take care of the teaching, as the whole focus of the letter demands, and to direct the life of the community. In this way 1 Tim 3:2 demands that they be «able to teach» and 1 Tim 5:17 (as 3:5 before) recommends they be able preside with some skill (even though it repeats that their main effort should be in «preaching and teaching»). Something similar we find in the first chapter of the letter to Titus: 1:7 (manages God's house) and 1:9 (hold firmly to the trustworthy message as it has been taught).

I repeat that these facts are widely known today. The New Testament does not know the structure soon to be found in the letters of Ignatius of Antioch taken in their current drafting[43]: there is no local chief in the community with strictly speaking episcopal powers, nor is there either an absolute distinction —with regards to power— between the monarchic «bishop» and the «priests»[44]. Whoever believes that the «Pastoral Epistles» were written

---

43 I say «in their current drafting» so as not to enter into the thesis of J. Rius Camps about the supposed later interpolation added to these letters precisely in the more «authoritarian» passages. On this point I am not qualified to give an opinion (cf. *The Four Authentic Letters of Ignatius The Martyr*, Rome: PIOS, 1980). I wonder if the explanation given by R. Brown of the most «authoritarian» passages of Ignatius would not make unnecessary Rius' hypothesis (cf. *La comunidad del discípulo amado*, Salamanca: Sígueme, 1983,) 150-151.

44 This indistinctiveness lasts at least until Saint Jerome who clearly identifies bishops and presbyters: «The Apostle teaches clearly that the presbyters are the same as the bishops...» (he continues to compare Acts 20:28 with Titus 1:5ff, etc.). «When subsequently one presbyter was chosen to preside over the rest, this was done to remedy schism and to prevent each individual from rending the Church of Christ by drawing it to himself» (*Epist ad Evangelium*: PL 22,1193 and 1194).

relatively early could argue that this is due to the fact that the Apostles still lived and they were the true «bishops» (this is why I said before that these questions were not theologically insignificant). Others argue that this monarchic bishop

«So, the presbyter is the same as the bishop and the churches were governed by a Council of Presbyters, until the time when by innuendo of the devil, passions started to appear in religion and people started to say: «I follow Paul, I follow Apollo, I follow Cephas» (1Cor 1:12). For once each one thought that those he baptized were «his» and not of Christ, it was decided everywhere that one of the bishops be put in charge of all the rest so he would care for the whole Church in order to eradicate the seed of schisms» (*Comentario a Tito* 1:1-5: PL 26,562).

Both texts seem to respond to historical facts and to the New Testament. That is why they provoke the question: if at a certain time it *was legitimate* to change in one direction to avoid schisms, would it not be legitimate at another moment to change in another direction —which in addition has the guarantee of tradition— when historical inertia has made of centralism or authoritarianism serious problems for the Church?

It is known that in the XVI Century both the Lutheran and the Calvinist churches used these texts to justify the ordination of pastors by other pastors (not bishops) «in situations of need». In this way, they argued, the apostolic succession had not been broken. And even though the Council of Trent declared that the difference between bishops and presbyters is that the first had the power to confer confirmation and ordination, the question of whether that difference corresponds to divine law or to ecclesial law was left open (cf. DS 1777, D 967). And, in fact, confirmation today is administered sometimes by priests with episcopal license but without episcopal consecration. In this way of proceeding, the churches of the Reform are less strange than it seems to us today, since the traces of such a point of view, inside the Catholic Church, seem to go back to a little before the Reformation: in the XV Century, two Popes granted power to confer ordination to people who were not bishops (Boniface IX, in 1400, to the abbot of Saint-Osith; and Martin V, in 1427, to the abbot of Altzelle: cf. DS 1145 and 1290). Both circumstances create serious difficulties to our way of thinking. It has even been said that those papal bulls were not valid, because the Pope had overstepped his power, or that *«conferre ordines»* only meant that the abbot *could call any bishop* even if it was not the ordinary... The most common answer is normally that the priests who received those powers could only ordain in a valid way in the cases mentioned in the pontifical indult, while a bishop could always ordain validly even if against the Pope's will. (Cf. LECUYER J., in collaboration with BARAUNA G., (dir.), *La Iglesia del Vaticano II*, I, Barcelona: Juan Flors, 1966; 884). Nonetheless, it is possible that this answer deserves a keener investigation. In recent times we have seen some «bizarre» ordinations (in Spain in El Palmar de Troya) and other illicit ones (in the schismatic group of Monsignor Lefebvre). I do not think that today there can be many who seriously consider the first ones valid. But maybe we have not reflected enough *about what is the element which logically makes those ordinations invalid, in spite of their being canonically correct*. Maybe from this a further question could arise that is of interest in these historical times: are we sure that the universal episcopal body with its Head does not have the power to declare the ordinations of Monsignor Lefebvre not only licit but also *invalid*? Or can we speak here also of a lack of «material» apostolicity in an extreme situation similar to that at the Council of Constance mentioned previously? Would this not have to do with the «intention of doing what the Church does», something considered necessary for any sacrament... This would liberate the Church from many false fears of «blackmail» that only serve to create difficulties for the Church's mission. Maybe it would only be convenient —by reason of the seriousness of the subject— that this decision were assumed, as we have said, by the «Universal episcopal body with its Head». I would like to mention, in ending this long note, that the false intention of doing what the Church does was given as a reason, at the time of Leo XIII, to declare invalid Anglican ordinations. And, nonetheless, to judge that intention about a happening of the past (as complex as we now see was the fact of the Reformation, too) is infinitely more difficult than to do it for something present.

is precisely Timothy or Titus and this is why they are the recipients of the letters. The argument, nonetheless, is weak, as neither of them is called «bishop» nor is the function of «feeding the sheep» (*poimanein* or *episkopein*) assigned to them in exclusivity. Perhaps it would be better to conclude, with G. Lohfink, that Timothy and Titus are «prototype of a responsible minister but not archetype of a bishop»[45]. His function, curiously, has no name by which it can be designated. And when, on another occasion —near in time and space to the «Pastoral Epistles»— the author of 1 Peter describes himself, he does so calling himself simply «an elder myself» (5:1)[46]. Also, the tone of the letters show that, even though they seem addressed to only one person, they are conceived to be read by the whole community: hence the present instructions about the diverse members of the community (slaves, women, etc.) and the concluding greetings «for you» in the plural or «with you all» (cf. 1 Tim 6:21; 2 Tim 3:22; Titus 3:15). We find ourselves then probably «on the way» towards a situation that will end up being the one described by Ignatius of Antioch, but without having reached it already. We should underline, on the one hand, that this situation is the fruit of a logical evolution of things and, on the other hand, that its last phase does not belong anymore to the New Testament, not even to that part of the New Testament written after the departure of the Apostles.

If until now we have spoken less of the second group, it is because what is more clear and more elaborate is what makes up the functions of the first group.

b) The deacons. This second group is mentioned immediately after the first one (1 Tim 3:8ff). Of their duties practically nothing is said; only their moral qualities are underlined. From the fact that it is recommended that they should not be «pursuing dishonest gain» some have deduced that the deacons were dedicated to the administration of the church's resources and for this reason were exposed to that temptation. We would then be in a situation like the one in Acts 6 which we already said was historically questionable. But probably it is not possible to reach such a concrete conclusion and we should limit ourselves to seeing the deacons as «auxiliaries» to the previous group.

---

45 «*Die Normativitat der Amtsvorstellungen in der Pastoralbriefen*» *Theol.Quart.*157 (1977) 93-106; summarized in *Selecciones de Teología* 17 (1978) 287-294.

46 Here, too, we find again the function of example mentioned before: the elders must be shepherds «not pursuing dishonest gain» nor «lording it», but «being examples to the flock» (vv. 2-5). These are details often forgotten.

I want to close this section with an acute observation by R. Brown that will help us not to convert the testimony of the «Pastoral Epistles» into something absolute or exclusive. If we had to stick *exclusively* to the qualities that are here proposed for the ministers of the Church, then Paul should have been excluded from ministry, because he did not possess some of those qualities[47]. This observation is more than a subtle dialectic balancing act. It hits on something that affects not only the nature itself of the ecclesial ministry but also the Church's present situation of crisis. For *the ministry cannot be the same in a missionary situation as in a situation of «settlement»*; in the former there is much more risk, while in the latter many will feel the temptation to «bury the talents». And what occurs in our Church today is that many Christians feel the need to return to a missionary Church precisely because in the present crisis of the world they see a missionary opportunity for the Church. On the other hand, many other Christians only feel the need to «secure and retain what one already has» (or the little there is left), because they perceive the present crisis of the world as a time of great danger for the Church, and against such a threat even the advice of the author of the «Pastoral Epistles» would be insufficient...[48]. The repeated conflicts of the present age between the Vatican and many religious Orders have sprung, in my opinion, from this very root.

---

[47] «Indeed, Paul might not have been able to meet several requirements the Pastorals would impose on the presbyter-bishops... Rough vitality and a willingness to fight bare-knuckled for the Gospel were part of what made Paul a great missionary, but such characteristics might have made him a poor residential community supervisor» (BROWN R., *The Churches The Apostles Left Behind,* New York: Paulist Press, 1984) 35. And further on: «...the thrust toward such highly prudential leaders, holding on to the past, creates an orientation that is not going to favour the innovations necessary for a dynamic missions. ...Alas, the judgment of both higher church authorities and of the laity on pastors has too often been exclusively along the lines promoted by the Pastorals» (BROWN R., *The Churches The Apostles Left Behind,* New York: Paulist Press, 1984, 42). The truth of this observation is highlighted by the present line of episcopal appointments over the world: one could say that today the «Pauls» are not chosen but only the «Timothies».

[48] In this sense one should add —in my opinion— that the papal trips are not properly missionary trips (how could they be otherwise in the conditions in which they are made?), but they wish to be, above all, a *strengthening of the ecclesiastical organization.* In them the Gospel is not announced (it is given as known or already announced), but instead «natural» or controversial principles of morality and imperatives for ecclesial identity. But what is important in these trips is not exactly the «announcement», but the movement of masses and the visual spectacle.

Finally in the «Pastoral Epistles» we find a more articulate structure (although maybe not complete) of the gesture of the laying on of the hands. Prior to this we had found that there was no laying of hands on Matthias when he was elected for the group of the Twelve, but Ananias does lay his hands on Paul before he baptized him (cf. Acts 1:26 and 9:17). This permits the suspicion that the laying on of hands was not codified at the beginning.

But now this gesture acquired for the community the character of a real «ordination». Timothy possesses a *charism* (not merely a «function») that has been *given* to him (not merely «recognized») *by* the imposition of hands by Paul (2 Tim 1:6) and by the council of elders (1 Tim 4:14). I do not believe we can use the difference in prepositions (*meta* in the second case and *dia* in the first) to suppose that in the first case we have a specific «ordination» at the hands of a bishop and in the second the «confirmation» on the part of the group of assisting elders, as is done in the present ordination of priests. I believe that this interpretation suffers from a certain «fundamentalism» which makes the texts say more than they pretend to do. The author of these letters seems to speak here more unconcernedly, and the only clear thing is that the «Pastoral Epistles» testify to the transmission of «responsible» ministry through a rite of imposition of hands which can be performed by the Apostle or by the «elders» of a given community. In turn, this rite is called upon to perpetuate itself as Titus is asked to «appoint elders» (Titus 1:5). And even though here the laying on of hands is not *expressly* mentioned, this seems to be taken for granted when we see that in 1 Tim 5:22 the recipient is counseled: «do not be hasty in the laying on of hands». Here it is logical to suppose that both phrases allude to the same thing, even if they differ in words.

In any case we find that the imposition of hands has been converted now to *the way of transmitting the charism for leading the community.* The ministry is considered here more «turned inwards» according to the tone of these letters. In Acts 13:3, on the contrary, the imposition of hands had a more «outward» character: it implied being «*sent* on their way by the Holy Spirit» (v.4) toward the world beyond the community. In the «Pastoral Epistles», on the other hand, it implies being constituted by the Holy Spirit as *the backbone of the community.*

Both meanings should not be set against each other, even though their difference is clear and permits again the understanding of two possible approaches to ecclesial ministry. That is why precisely —and this will be our last observation in

Chapter 2

81

this brief analysis— it seems strange that all through the «Pastoral Epistles» there is no mention *at all* of the relationship between ministry and presiding at the Eucharist: not even when the tasks of the bishops-elders are mentioned (which we saw in the last section) nor when they speak about the laying on of hands.

In conclusion we can say three things:

a) That longstanding Old Testament gesture, which has its anthropological basis as a demonstration of trust and welcome[49], has received a new meaning which we can define as: *trust in ecclesial service* (transmitting it so). Here is noted the ecclesial character of the ministry, which gives this work its title, the ministers are effectively «builders of the community». Notwithstanding the fact that these «people of the community» can assume different tasks inwardly («Pastoral Epistles») or outwardly (*Acts of the Apostles*).

b) This evolution which is certainly *very logical* probably safeguarded the early Church's identity at the time of its consolidation. It is an achievement which should be retained and the «Pastoral Epistles» should not be reviled for this as examples of conservatism or as an instance of an «early Catholicism». No community can survive purely on spontaneity. The same ecclesial communities born of the Reformation had to end up writing their own «Pastorals», each one in its own way. Formal apostolicity may not be enough by itself (as we mentioned already) but it is absolutely advisable.

c) Nonetheless, to say that this evolution is logical does not mean to defend that such evolution be dogmatically necessary and unchangeable. This achievement in the consolidation of the community seems to have sprung from the problematic situation itself of the early Church. There is no indication authorizing it to be said that it proceeds from some norm or legislation given in advance by Jesus himself. Or to quote Brown again: «The fact, however, that the Pastorals were shaped by the problem then at hand often has not been recognized, and they have been thought to describe an ideal church order adequate for all times. In fact they make no structural provision for on-going missionary activity»[50].

---

49 And that had been used by Jesus himself (cf. Mt 19:15; Mark 6:5)

50 BROWN R., *The Churches The Apostles Left Behind*, New York: Paulist Press 1984, 41-42. On the norms of the «Pastoral Epistles» see also the article mentioned in footnote 45, against the idea of H. Schlier, who in fact presents the «Pastoral Epistles» as the only ecclesial norms. According to Lohfink, to take these Epistles as normative would imply the norm of the marriage of ministers. What is normative in the «Pastoral Epistles» is what is affected by the concepts of *parathêke* or *didaskalia*. I present his conclusions according to the translation of *Selecciones de Teología*: «God trusted his gospel to Paul, Paul trusted it as *parathêke* to Timothy and Titus and these

The necessity of being an «alternative community» and the tension toward that goal

Adaptation to the situation (Jerusalem), missionary creativity (Antioch), charismatic plurality (Pauline churches), fraternal equality (Johannine communities), authority in times of crisis («Pastoral Epistles»)… These are some of the diverse configurations the ecclesial ministry acquired already in the limited region of the New Testament and which are models for the Church.

With a certain overarching effort, we can now indicate that there is a last point that is common to all the churches of the New Testament, although to study it we will limit ourselves to the Gospel of Matthew[51], given the summary character this work seems to have. I refer to the obligation the ecclesial ministers have (and all Christians) to mould the Church as «alternative community», and that is in line with the exemplary nature of the ministry we have already seen.

The expression «alternative community» sometimes raises certain misgivings, because it could suppose that the Church pretends to «replace» the world[52]. This is why we must hasten to make clear that our formula means the same as «sacrament of salvation», typical of Vatican II. *Visible signs* (sacraments) of salvation can only exist if it is shown that there are *possible alternatives* (even if partial) to the no-salvation situation. And to show that these possibilities exist is why, in the New Testament, Luke emphasizes the «communist» organization of the first church in Jerusalem (cf. Acts 2:43-47; 4:32-36). And Paul supports the charismatic weaving of his churches as an expression that the real community

Chapter 2

83

---

in turn to others. It is then a succession of *doctrine*, of teaching and not of ministerial power… The Pastoral Epistles know that without a minister in the local churches the transmission of the gospel is not possible. That is why they speak so much of the ministry. But this is not to establish set structures of the ministry, but to guarantee the faithful transmission of the *parathêke*… If we could ask the author of the Pastoral Epistles if what he really wanted was a specific ministerial structure as norm for the Church, he would answer: «No, I do not want a specific *ministry*, but the *gospel* as the norm of the Church. The task is yours to create the *ministry* that can be the best guarantee of the transmission and realization of the gospel»…» LOHFINK G., «La normatividad de la concepción del ministerio en las cartas pastorales» in *Selecciones de Teología* 17 (1978). 293-294.

51 For the community of Mark, cf. ALEGRE X., «El movimiento de Jesús y las primeras comunidades cristianas» in Misión Abierta, 5-6 (1987), 36-40.

52 Such suspicions were formulated some time ago against *La Alternativa Cristiana* by CASTILLO J.M. and, more recently, against *La Iglesia que Jesús quería* by LOHFINK G. This author talks perfectly well of a «community of contrast». Jon Sobrino says, for this purpose, that he believes (at least for the Latin American Church) the expression «leavening community» to be more precise.

is not made and imposed from above, but by communion in diversity. And the Johannine churches took so long to accept the essential ecclesial authority because they thought it compromised Christian fraternity...

This obsession to show that fraternity (Luke), equality (John) and liberty (Paul) are possible, or that in Jesus Christ there are no more lord or slave, man or woman, Jew or Greek, etc., was present in different ways in almost all of the New Testament. But this necessary obsession already in the New Testament comes up against the hardness of reality and with the set ways of the sinners who take advantage of liberty and equality to affirm their own selfishness.

So, it seems to have been the evangelist Matthew who best achieved the synthesis between both principles, the *alternative community* and the *community of this world*[53]. Matthew clearly establishes the authority of the ecclesial ministry, but at the same time tries to establish with equal clarity the limits and conditions of that authority. In the same way that he had understood that it was possible to save Judaism while condemning the Jews of his time, he will now establish the possibility of saving authority while condemning «religious» ways of exercising it. This is the point we still have to review and for that we will mainly use chapter 18 of his Gospel.

6.1. THE THREE NOVELTIES OF CHRISTIAN MINISTRY

Chapter 18 of Matthew presents many of what can be considered «authentic words» of Jesus. But put in such a way that they have all the signs of being editorial work done by the evangelist. That is why we should pay attention especially to the work of composition (reflected above all in the *scheme* of the chapter) in order to discover its lessons. And this editorial work seems to have ordered Jesus' words in three important teaching sections:

a) *Christian authority has nothing to do with «being the greatest»* (Mt 18:1-9).

The whole chapter is framed by this expression and the evangelist will underline specifically that this is a criteria «of the Kingdom» (cf. v.3). To the pretension of being the greatest is opposed «becoming like children» (vv. 3-4). Increasingly exegetes agree that the child is not presented as model of innocence but as an example of smallness and even of little consideration[54], of «humilia-

---

53 Cf. AGUIRRE R., «La Iglesia Cristiana de Antioquía de Siria» in RLT 10 (January-April 1987), 81.

54 Cf., for example, BONNARD P., *El Evangelio según San Mateo* (Madrid: Cristiandad, 1983), 389: «In Palestine at the time of Jesus, as in the ancient world in general, the child is a weak being without pretensions, whose humility is more social than subjective; the child has nothing to say in society and is limited to obeying the orders received; just like the *poor* in Matthew, the only

tion» (v. 4). Stretching the comparison, in a small digression provoked by the theme of the scandal of the «little ones»[55], the evangelist suggests that «becoming like children» can signify even «to cripple oneself» (cf. vv. 8-9). This supposes the greatest reversal of earthly power, which rather always implies «self-aggrandisement». These words of verses 8-9 are clearly taken out of their context in Jesus to reinforce the lesson Matthew wishes to give.

b) *Christian authority has to do, most of all, with universality and, because of it, with the «excluded»* (Mt 18:10-14).

The mention of children leads easily to think of the lost, of those outside... And immediately Matthew introduces the parable of the lost sheep (vv. 10-14) which has also been taken out of the context in which Jesus presented it and ends with an expression which also appeared in the preceding epigraph: «one of these little ones...» (cf. v. 14 with v. 6).

We must value the creativity and daring this change of context supposes: what Jesus seems to have said in his behavior with the social outcast is applied now by Matthew to the conduct of the ecclesial ministry: «For the Son of man came to save the lost» (v. 11)[56]. In order to value the daring of this evangelist it would be enough to think that perhaps on no other point throughout history has ecclesiastical authority been so little faithful to Jesus as on *this point* precisely. The classical themes of simony, luxury, Nicolaisim[57], earthly power... have in reality been *minor* infidelities in comparison to that tendency to live and act «for themselves and for their own more than for those that are lost», and to be happy more for those who have remained than for those who have been brought back (this here has more to do with *universality* than with those materially *poor*): a tendency which throughout history has produced so many breaks in Christian unity. The thing is that worldly authorities are always authorities of a faction (a party, a social class, etc.). Christian authority and ministry, on the other hand, should be *of all* and, precisely because of this, of the most remote. How very difficult this is and how, too, it tends to encounter great resistance from the «sheep» who describe themselves as faithful!

---

thing a child can do is «receive» with joy whatever is offered». This is also suggested in the preceding line (35b) in the parallel passage in Mark (9:36).

55 Matthew connects this scandal with the theme presented earlier of the *little ones*, suppressing the intermediate verses which appear in Mark 9:38-41.

56 This verse is missing in some codices because it does not seem to fit with what comes before. However, the connection can be grasped if we consider the children as marginalized.

57 A heresy or sect mentioned in Revelation 2:6-15, the contents of which are uncertain.

c) *Authority in the Church should only be a last resort* (Mt 18:15-20).

Following the parable of the lost sheep, Matthew proposes a series of behavioral norms which seem to underline the validity of the intermediate resorts, even in the field that could be more decisive: crime. Each one should go to look for his *own* «lost sheep», too, or lost *for that person*, instead of turning to the authority to exclude them. And everyone should look for them even without having any kind of coercive power or legitimacy to take justice into their hands. But they must be looked for through fraternal dialogue, understanding how much more valuable it is «to win the brother» (v. 15) than to vindicate oneself.

But it happens to us that we are not sufficiently free, brotherly and humble to carry out that fraternal correction as it should be done and we frequently turn it into a more aggressive offensive. Hence we prefer to fall back on authority, through betrayal or anonymous denunciation. Jesus proposes another way infinitely more noble and humane, where the action of authority is only the last resource. All this we can affirm even without entering into the two exegetically debated issues in this passage: what the word *ekklesía*[58] means and to whom the words of verse 18 may be directed[59]. Leaving aside the exegetical discussion, the proposal of a way more fraternal than authoritarian is clear. And the evangelist adds an impressive reason: *Jesus Christ is there where brotherhood begins, even if it is only between two or three* (vv. 19-20). Matthew does not say that Christ is there where order is established, even as necessary and important as this sometimes is (cf. v. 18): «recognized in heaven»[60].

Furthermore, we have to add that these three observations affect not only authority, but *all members* of the community. If the components of the community live with each one trying to be «the greatest», if they live centered upon themselves and with more inclination toward victory than fraternal dialogue,

---

58 The universal Church? The community of Jerusalem? The community of Antioch which, according to many, is the community in which Matthew writes? And also, the totality of these communities or only the leaders? etc., etc.

59 The dominant opinion is that Jesus is speaking to all the disciples (cf. 18:1: *oi mathêtai*). However, see, for example, Matthew 10:1; 11:1, where the «disciples» mentioned are expressly the Twelve (*tous dôdeka mathêtas*).

60 All commentators show great surprise at the expxressions used by Matthew in the sentence: «treat them as you would a pagan or a tax collector», since precisely both terms designate the object of a particular benevolence of Jesus («friend of tax collectors», etc.). This is why I dare to suggest that the phrase «treat them as you would a pagan or a tax collector» does not exactly mean: treat them as someone excluded and deserving of condemnation, but rather: treat them as someone to be retrieved.

then authority will tend to consider itself as elevation, to focus on self-centeredness and to proceed in an authoritarian way.

d) *Conclusion and the foundation of this conduct: God is Forgiveness.*

The last touch of this editorial work is that Matthew closes the chapter by introducing precisely the parable of the unmerciful servant (vv. 23-31), by which he is telling us that the basis of all that came before is that God's authority is *Pardon* while human authority (the authority of the servant whose debt had been forgiven) tends to be *violence*. Catholic liturgy is enormously profound when it prays «*omnipotentiam Tuam parcendo maxime et miserando manifestas*» (the omnipotence of God is manifested above all through forgiveness and mercy). Hopefully this *lex orandi* will become in us Christians a little *lex vivendi*, too.

In short: because Jesus reveals an «alternative» God (not power but love), the authority of the Church should also be alternative and the Church is called to be an alternative community as an indispensable starting point for its mission.

6.2. THE CONTRAST WITH THE RELIGIOUS AUTHORITIES

One should add that what Matthew proposes as rules of conduct in Chapter 18 is enlightened still more by the denunciations in the rest of his Gospel directed towards the «Jewish» way of exercising authority: the way of the Scribes and Pharisees… Probably the expression «Scribes and Pharisees» responds more to the historical context in which Matthew writes rather than the context in which Jesus lived and pronounced such criticisms. That is why in the title of this section I have referred more to «religious» authority in general. In any case, «Matthew is aware that, left on their own, the authoritative figures would inevitably begin to act like the scribes and Pharisees». And through the attacks of Jesus on the Jewish authorities Matthew corrects those burgeoning attitudes in the Church. To counteract such danger, he will insist on the idea that the Church should govern *not only in the name of Jesus, but also in the the spirit of Jesus*[61].

This criticism of «religious» authority could be reduced to two points:

a) imposing unnecessary loads which they themselves are unwilling to bear (cf. Mt 23:3-4 and also Peter's speech in Acts 15:10). Luke's clamor is very expressive: «But you are not to be like that!» (Luke 22:26);

b) acting in order to be seen and praised, occupying the first places and holding honorary titles (cf. Mt 23:5-12 and note the appearance of the «to be seen»

---

61 BROWN R., *The Churches The Apostles Left Behind*, New York, Paulist Press, 1984, 1980, 136 and 138.

as well in the censure of Pharisee religiousness in Mt 6:1ff.). Luke 22 had said «call themselves benefactors».

From this so deeply human double source spring a series of behavioral actions which the rest of Matthew's Chapter 23 will denounce, and all of them deserve the same expression: an authority which acts in agreement with those two principles mentioned will be a *hypocritical* authority. And its hypocrisy will consist in:

a) lying with subtle juridical distinctions (vv. 16-22: «swear by»…);

b) observing detailed regulations in order to forget the great virtues (vv. 23-34: the gnat before the camel and the tithe before mercy and justice);

c) cleaning the outside, leaving what is inside dirty (vv. 25-28: «whited sepulchers»);

d) incapacity to recognize by word the sins shown by their own works (29ff.: «build the sepulchers of the prophets they did slay»);

e) ending by «shutting the kingdom of heaven» (vv. 13-15: which they assert they open and on which pretend to justify their power).

The enormous seriousness of these observations by Matthew, expressed, too, with striking force and beauty, was already perceived by Saint Jerome when, in his commentary on this passage, he had the courage to write: «miserable of us on to whom have passed these vices of the Pharisees…!»[62]. Because of this the ministers and authorities in the churches would do well to look with profound respect on these words as words directed to *ourselves* (which is what they are), more than traces of a totally obsolete past which does not affect us at all. Matthew thought that the Church could be more unfaithful to the lordship of Jesus *by the way of exercising* authority (very much needed, on the other hand) than *by the absence* of it. This is why the temptation for our Church today could be in clearly accepting all the (necessary) recovery of authority which Matthew presents, without at the same time incorporating all the correctives and conversions which the spirit of Jesus imposes on authority. This pretension of the «*alter Christus*» without the «*alter Iesus*» (as we formulated above) could end in what R. Brown calls «the Caiaphas principle»: the false appeal to people to justify conduct which defends the interests of power[63].

---

62 «*Vae nobis miseris ad quos phariseorum vitia transierunt!*» (PL 26, 168).

63 «So often churches work on what I call «the Caiaphas principle» when they encounter a brilliantly disturbing leader: It is better that one man be eliminated than that the whole institution perish (John 11:50). There may be a certain societal inevitability to that principle, but the source of it should at least make the designation «weakness» none too strong for a tendency (which is

7
New Testament conclusions

᧞

7.1. FROM THE HISTORICAL PERSPECTIVE

One suspects that in the churches of the New Testament an evolution like this must have taken place: the «presbyteral» structure of the church at Jerusalem (which imitated the Jewish way of organization) would have passed, during the Christian mission, to groups of communities with a very charismatic organization, but polarized by the outstanding personality of some «Apostle» or charismatic itinerant. When these started to die the «presbyteral» form would have been reborn, but now with some «co-presbyter» who was a sort of *«primus inter pares»*. And from this the stage had been set to move to a monarchical episcopate as we repeatedly find in the letters of Ignatius of Antioch[64].

7.2. FROM THE THEOLOGICAL PERSPECTIVE

Some conclusions emerge.

7.2.1. *JESUS LEFT THE CHURCH SIMPLY THE «APOSTOLATE»*

This institution shows the need and ecclesial character of the ministry. The Church needs people for the mission of the community and people to help the life of that missionary community. In other words: the Church is a sent community, not a closed one, and fraternal, not hierarchical. But within that community there is a group of persons, *ultimately*[65] *responsible for the mission,* who discern and clarify the life and activity of the community, according to the needs

---

incipient in the Pastorals) to favour blandness» (BROWN R., *The Church The Apostles Left Behind,* New York, Paulist Press, 1984) 42,.

We find another example of this way of proceeding in the criteria used in the trial of the famous Bishop Carranza I already mentioned earlier: «Once they arrested a person, even if there were no grounds, something against that person should be presented so it would not seem the arrest were done lightly». Evidently «it is less inconvenient that someone suffer than to make the authority and its office suspect». Both citations, cf. GONZÁLEZ FAUS J.I., *Proyecto de hermano. Visión creyente del hombre,* Santander: Sal Terrae, 2000³, 191.

64 On the other hand, 1 Clement (dated *c.* 95) which establishes very clearly the principle we call «formal» apostolicity (the apostles, where they preached, would establish *«episkopous kai diakonous»,* who in their turn named other successors), seems to reflect still the same organization of the presbyteral council we saw in the «Pastoral Epistles» (Cf. 1Clement 42, 44, 47).

65 Ultimately means that they are not alone: since all the members of the community share in that responsibility in some way.

of the mission. This could be the meaning of the institution of the «Apostolate» the Church receives from Jesus[66].

But Jesus left the Church a sufficiently free field to shape itself in the most appropriate manner to respond to the different challenges of the mission, which is the true mandate of the Lord (cf. Mt 28:19-20 and parallels). Among these was also the decisive challenge of the succession of the Apostles. And to respond to such challenges the Church used both «social» models already in existence (Jewish presbyteral model) and models from its own experience of the Apostles with Jesus (the apostolic college and the primacy of Peter).

7.2.2. THE TASKS GRADUALLY PLACED ON THE FIRST CHURCH MINISTERS

They fit, perhaps, into this triple field: to teach, help and coordinate (or lead), which, in turn, is not too distant from the tasks Bloch identifies for all people or communities on the march. And yet we can add a brief word about each one.

We will begin emphasizing that these tasks can easily be assimilated to the classical «triple power» (of Teacher, King and Priest), while maintaining the ambiguity of the term «priest» between the cultic and supportive. And we should add that these three words can only be read in their *Christological* meaning and not in their worldly meaning. To appeal, for example, to the royalty of Christ to justify the temporal power of the popes is one of the atrocities committed throughout history and shows the dangers of these false, non-Christological readings. Royalty, from a Christological understanding, consists in «giving testimony to the truth» instead of imposing it (Jn 18:37) and to reign «from the cross» («*regnavit a lingo Deus*» chanted the ancient liturgy). Priesthood consists in «offering oneself» and not in cultic offerings (all the testimony of the *Letter to the Hebrews* we saw in the previous chapter). And teaching does not consist so much in universal laws as in the proclamation of the Kingdom and, so, the will of God for each person and particular situation, which sometimes will be more demanding than general laws.

---

66 According to J. Roloff, Luke «totally agrees [on this point] with the Pauline idea of apostolic ministry, which —according to Rom 1:1; 1 Cor 15:10; and Gal 1:15— essentially consists in being ordered and sent by the Risen One to give witness to the Gospel». (Cf. ROLOFF J., *Hechos de los Apótoles*, Madrid, Cristianidad, 1984, 60). And witness to the Gospel is given by proclaiming it explicitly (missionary work) and living in community in accordance with it («alternative community»).

Having provided this summary, we can explain in a little more detail the tasks described:

a) «To teach» means, *at the same time*, to safeguard *and* to transmit, to preserve *and* to realize, to maintain *and* to make clear What has sometimes been called the Catholic «and» in opposition to Protestantism, must be applied here, too. Because the Christian «deposit» is *living*, and it is preserved only when it is maintained «to be handed on». This duality has its risks, but greater still is the risk of preserving it literally unchanged, as if it were a corpse. The Jewish Christians and Paul, with his daring and creativity, were more faithful to Jesus' deposit than the first community of «converted Pharisees» in Jerusalem.

b) «To help» is an «integral» task referring both to the material and to the spiritual, without it being possible to oppose or create a dilemma about both tasks. From the very beginning, ecclesial ministry has to do *also* with the distribution of bread (Acts 6:1ff.). Spiritual help is perfectly described in Acts 14:22 (*episteridsontes tas psychas*) as a «strengthening of believing spirits». By its very nature this includes a two-dimensional difficult teaching: to console and to demand at the same time.

c) In relation to co-ordination or leadership, the decisive mission is to maintain the unity of the community in the midst of the inevitable and necessary plurality of its members. To encourage the communion between those who are different more than to impose one's own particular way is the mission of the Christian ministry[67]. In the community nobody is lord of anybody, in the same way that nobody is the property of anybody (of Paul, of Apollos, of Cephas…, cf. 1 Cor 1:12). And this is applicable not only to groups or persons among themselves but also to their ministers. Because all have «but one God and one Lord» (1 Cor 8:6). This is why I have said several times that the expression «*in persona Christi*» as a designation of the ministry has the great danger that the minister may confuse the personality of Christ with their own personality… And it will only be applied correctly if the minister has entered

[67] «In essentials, unity; in doubtful things, liberty; in all things, charity». This well-known Augustinian principle is the one that today is seriously threatened by all the «Judaeo-Palestinians» of our Church who cannot stand what is doubtful and only seem to want their own security and comfort from the Church. And so they read the Augustinian formula in this other way: «Unity much further away than what is necessary, the line of thought of the superior when in doubt and restrictive measures in all». (And one should note that those Judaeo-Palestinians generally have preferential hearing at the time of the appointment of superiors). But such a Church will never be a community in which the alternative character of all that belongs to Jesus will shine.

before «*in persona Iesu*» (which implies the «de-personalization» of oneself more than the imposition of one's own will).

7.2.3. THE NEW TESTAMENT SAYS NOTHING ABOUT THE RELATIONSHIP OF THE CHURCH'S MINISTERS TO THE CHURCH'S WORSHIP

After this outline of the tasks of the ecclesial ministry, the absence of information in the New Testament about the relationship of the Church's ministers to worship is striking. This is marked not only with respect to the terminology (as we have said already), but also with respect to the concrete *tasks*. James (5:14ff.) has left us a brief reference to the prayer of the «elders» over the sick, anointing them with oil, and maybe this falls more into a chapter on «care of the sick» than a chapter concerned specifically with «worship». John (20:23) has preserved for us a hint of the power to forgive sins. But about the way of structuring this role (as well as the *structure* of the celebrations of the Lord's Supper)[68] the New Testament has not left us any testimony, except, perhaps, the controversial phrase in Acts 20:11 where it says of the Apostle Paul that he «broke the bread».

7.2.4. IN SEARCH OF THE «LEAVENING COMMUNITY»

In the performance of these tasks, both the minister and the community must take seriously before history the charge of trying to be «alternative community» or «leavening community». This presupposes *not superiority* but indeed *greater responsibility* for the Christians, precisely because Christian mission must not impose anything, but only offer the Good News. Today, this implies for the ecclesial ministry the grave obligation that whoever discharges it be a person of unquestionable ecclesiology (as clear as possible) and, at the same time, a person profoundly respectful of the «image of God» and the divine dignity of all human beings. A respect in itself religious and which should translate into the smallest details of daily existence.

---

68 Of whose existence on the other hand we do have testimony (cf. 1Cor 11:17ff.). But what is said there in relation to its structure is that the Eucharist is not compatible with the scandalous differences in the way of life in which «some go hungry while others are drunk».

Within this frame we have to repeat that the New Testament leaves the Church *today* great freedom to mould itself according to the present demands of the mission. A freedom which springs from the variety and adaptability the ministries of the churches of the New Testament have shown us. The shaping of the different ecclesial ministries can aspire today to a «communion in diversity». And to maintain that communion the New Testament already offers a reference point, privileged mediation of the following of Jesus: the poor. The respect toward the poor, the preferential option (personal and structural) for them, which all —«Jews and Greeks»— have today as an integral element of their ministry «to remember the poor» (Gal 2:10) is one of the things which would most contribute to giving the Church that character of «alternative community» we saw in the previous conclusion.

Chapter 2

93

After all these conclusions, we should add that the present aspiration to substitute the duality «clerics-laity» with «community-ministries» is revealed as profoundly based on the New Testament... And binding for the whole of the Church today. I have mentioned elsewhere that what makes the one-sidedness of our Church, today, is that it seems to be built exclusively upon a Christology from John and an ecclesiology from the «Pastoral Epistles»[69]. This particularity is what we have to overcome appealing to the totality (that is, *cath-olicity*) of the New Testament. Even if that overcoming has been taking place since Vatican II, in reference to Christology, it remains unaltered, however, as regards ecclesiology.

We still have to see if it is possible to derive some lessons from the evolution of the ecclesial ministry throughout ecclesial tradition and history.

---

[69] Cf. GONZÁLEZ FAUS J.I., *La interpelación de las iglesias latinoamericanas a la Europa postmoderna*, Madrid: Fundación Santa María, 1988, 84-87.

The Clericalization of the Ministry

N.B. The development we are about to trace picks up, above all, that line of thought which, in fact, materialized and imposed itself. In practice, this line (which as such is only discernable today) co-exists with a thousand other aims from right or left which in the end did not succeed. So, for example, the letter of Pliny the Younger to Trajan (*c.* 112 A.D.) speaks about his having «tortured some slaves they [the Christians] called *deaconesses*». The *Apostolic Constitutions* (*c.* 380), in chapter VIII, seem to introduce a woman in the hierarchy, but in spite of the great influence they commanded, they ended up being condemned in the 7th century. The *Didaskalia* (*c.* 230), too, reflects a more organized and clerical church than the ones in the first and second Centuries; but the structure it describes is not the one that prevailed in history (cf. II,26,3-8, where it equates the figure of the bishop to the Father, that of the deacon to Christ and that of the deaconess to the Holy Spirit, while the priests, clearly undervalued in their work, are equated to the apostles, and the widows and orphans to the altar… Evidently this is not the order that triumphed in the end).

On the other hand, the significance of history is often ambiguous and so it is common to find historians disagreeing on the interpretation of the same data. An authoritarian way of proceeding, for example, does not reveal or mean the same thing when it takes place in a terribly hierarchical environment as when it takes place in a very democratic one. And on the contrary, a demeanor of freedom does not have the same interpretation or the same value when it takes place in a «hierarchical» situation as when it happens in a situation of authentic freedom. But of history we know and perceive much more about isolated facts than *global settings*. We tend to read data from our own world or perspective. The majority of the information we will resort to is, therefore, ambiguous, but ambiguous in *both ways*. This means that if it is not decisive proof for many modern aspirations, nor is it proof (and maybe less so) for time-honored theses.

This curious detail is an example of how history is almost always manipulated by the inevitable partiality of our access to it: the known *Enchiridion* of C. Kirch, which gathers the sources of the history of the early church and has been of use in so many seminaries and theological schools for decades, when speaking about the *Statuta Ecclesiae Antiqua* only records one canon from it about the wedding celebration, in which it is recommended that the couple be presented by their godparents and that they refrain from sexual intercourse on the night of the nuptial blessing.

Without undervaluing the good intentions of this canon, whoever has read this small work (in ML 56, as an appendix to Saint Leo), must have found in it other more significant, important and challenging canons for today, such as the one prohibiting

the Church from receiving donations or money from those who oppress the poor…
All the manuals (beginning with Denzinger itself) are full of this type of example. And
so, by the inevitable silences and the necessary preferences, a mindset is shaped, believed to be «traditional» when maybe it is only «purified».

I know perfectly well that something of the sort can happen with the historical summary presented here. That is why its conclusions are less definitive than some would
like. But I think that maybe it highlights *real* but at the same time *forgotten* aspects.

That the Church gradually became more structured as it left the New Testament and entered into history is to be expected of an institution which grew
amidst persecution and extended at a striking pace throughout the whole
oikoumené. What is surprising is that this structuring was to adopt the form of
«clericalization». This is not a late process which only started in the second mil-
lennium, as sometimes is implied, but something that was already taking place
in the first 6 centuries of the Church.

1

Functions in «the place» («Kleros») of the Lord

The first detail we should underline is that in the first two centuries of the
Church there are no «laymen», because there is no clergy either. At that time,
the word «clergy» retains its etymologic meaning (that is, lot that corresponds
by chance) and designates in this way *the whole lot* of the Lord, the whole Church.
It is substantially equivalent to the *people* of God. The word «layman», as such,
does not seem to have any application in the Church. It is used only once (I
Clem 40:5), but in a text that describes what used to happen in the Old Testament and has been superseded by Christ.

This does not mean that Clement did not have a clear awareness of authority and the Apostolate (even more with the need to resolve the secession
that had taken place in Corinth). To vindicate the need for authority, Clement
makes use of what happened in Israel and also what happens in civil society
(cf. 37:1-3). But it does not seem that this awareness has to rely on the distinction
between a *clergy* making up the strictly speaking ecclesiastic portion and a laity
«secular» in ecclesial matters. And the reason for this fact is stated in this way by
the author we are using: for those churches, the centrality of God and of Christ

is such that it does not admit the presence of any other human «center» and so it does not permit community functions to be the «priority of any human institution which centralizes them in order to delegate them afterwards»[1].

Some testimony has been preserved about these functions, especially thanks to the defenses or descriptions of the primitive Eucharists[2]. These speak about «lectors», about a «president of the brothers» (*tô proestoti tôn adelphôn*) to whom the offerings are presented, after which he recites the Eucharistic prayer and gives out food and alms to the needy, and about some «deacons» who distributed the bread and wine after the prayer of the aforementioned president. This latter is never called «priest», «celebrant», «elder» or «bishop», and it is possible that this linguistic detail has some theological meaning. Furthermore, there is no indication in these texts of a Eucharistic presidency established as a *uniform function*, something which is not found in Irenaeus, either[3]. Something else along these lines is revealed in 1 Clem 44:4 where there is reference to the fact that the removed presbyters in Corinth «had offered gifts piously» (particularly considering the attitude of this letter in relation to the fact that in all areas of reality everything has its function). But the only clear testimony in this matter is, as far as I know, Ignatius of Antioch's when he writes to the Smyrneans: «only consider valid that Eucharist which is celebrated by the Bishop or the person he appoints»[4]. This text merits a brief comment for two reasons:

a) Because it reflects a need in relation to the Church controlling the Eucharistic celebration. A need which extended to the very validity of the Eucharist; and an understandable need since it was vital to be able to ensure that the Eucharist was celebrated as Eucharist «of the Church», *recognized by the latter as its own* or «official». Irenaeus at that time gives an indication of some bizarre

---

1 FAIVRE A., *Les laïcs aux origines de l'Église*, (Paris: Le Centurion, 1984), 57. I have taken much information from this author, as also from his previous study: *Naissance d'une hiérarchie* (Editions Beauchesne, Paris 1977).

2 The defenses were born for apologetic reasons, in order to exonerate Christian Eucharists from pagan accusations about their being incestuous orgies where children were sacrificed, etc., etc. (As an example, cf. Justin, *Apology* I: 65-67). The descriptions look more at the interior life of the community (example: *Didaché*, chapter 9).

3 This also is logical given the purpose, apologetic more than juridical, of these texts. About Irenaeus, cf. *Adv.Haer*, IV, 17:5; IV, 18:4-5; V, 2:2-3. The theological problem of the Eucharist for Irenaeus is not to determine *who* celebrates (he always speaks in a general way of «the Church»), but to show that the Eucharist is not offered because God is «concupiscent or desirous of what is another's» and that the Eucharistic transformation opens up the possibility of the transformation of our bodies in the resurrection.

4 *Smyrn*. VIII, 1. It is not mentioned here either if it is a Eucharistic presidency assigned as *a habitual situation* or only *ad casum*. In Ignatius' text the first can only be affirmed of the Bishop.

forms of Eucharistic celebration by the Gnostics, and which —alluding to a similar problem the Church had with the gospels— we could label «apocryphal»[5]. And the pagan accusations we mentioned in footnote 87 would also call for some form of control. Ignatius himself delivers his norm after referring to some who «do not confess that the Eucharist is the flesh of the Savior» (VIII, 1).

b) Also because it already hints at the link between the presidency of the Eucharist and the presidency of the community, since immediately before the quoted phrase he has said: «Let no one do anything connected with the Church without the bishop». In subsequent centuries, this merging between the two was to take place very clearly.

But following our line of thought we must conclude that even though Ignatius had already posed the problem of the *right* to the Eucharistic presidency, three other testimonies (Justin, Irenaeus and the *Didaché*) only seem to bear witness to the *fact* of such presidency[6]. Their interest has gone down other routes: the structure of the celebration, the prayers said in it, the real presence and the fact that the Eucharist replaces all the old sacrifices, because it is celebrated by «the true high priestly race of God»[7]. And this detail is significant.

Apart from this we just have another pair of testimonies which tell us something about the language and the writing about the ministry which we are going to refer to in order to conclude this first part.

a) Almost by chance, the *Didaché* bears out the existence of «Apostles and prophets» (XI, 3-6); and mentions them to say that they shouldn't be given hospitality for more than a day or two and, when sending them on their way, they should be given bread but no money, because if they ask for it they are «false prophets». This swift sketch is more surprising because the *Didaché* is a work concerned with Christian hospitality (cf. XII, 1ff.). Thus it reveals that abuses on the part of the prophets had started already: the early «charis-

---

5 Cf. *Adv. Haer*, 1, 13, 2.

6 It is not possible to interpret the words of Justin (1, 67) —«the president raises prayers *ose dynamis autó*»— as if he were alluding to the power of priestly ordination. J. Solano expressly admits that he is forcing the translation of the text to make it say that: «The explanation of this phrase is debated. We give a translation that favors the interpretation that Saint Justin refers here to the *sacramental power* the president of the meeting should have in order to consecrate the body of the Lord» (SOLANO J., *Textos eucarísticos primitivos,* Madrid: BAC, 1952, 63; underlined by author). In the long run such procedures —in a text expressly admitted as under discussion— do not help but injure the Church, since only the truth sets us free.

7 Cf., viz., Justin, *Dialogue…* 116, 3.

matic travelers» were turning into «undercover free riders». It is the tough inertia of history…

The *Didaché* also charges the communities with electing inspectors and helpers (*epikopous kai diakonous,* xv, 1-3). And it tells us that they «perform the ministry of prophets and teachers» (*didáskolos,* which is probably the same as the «Apostles» in xi, 3). So they are ministries which differ from the ones in the previous paragraph not because of their field of action, but for the *immediate or mediate* character of their work. The author recommends that they choose «gentle, disinterested and proven» men (xv, 1). It is the first testimony that I know of about the *obligation to choose* the ministers in the community.

b) In the same way Justin, in his *Apologies,* alludes more than once to «Doctors» who act with a certain autonomy. According to Faivre, «the Apologies of Justin still reveal that spirit of free initiative». And probably it was only when the doctors stopped being autonomous that they started calling them «catechists»[8].

There is not much more to say. But this 2nd century situation deserved to be highlighted because, immediately, we are going to find at the start of the 3rd century a Copernican revolution in two of the points developed: in the first place, there is going to be a *concentration on the ministers of the Eucharistic celebration* (who will then be the «classical»: bishop, presbyter and deacon); and secondly we will see a *generalized appearance of the word «layman»* (in Clement of Alexandria, in Tertullian, in the Didaskalia of Syria, or in letters from Rome…) to designate those who do not belong to this triad. Here we find a situation very similar to ours which we should examine in more detail.

Before that I would like to make a quick summary of the 2nd century: in it we find presidents of the Eucharist who are so more as «a fact»; there are presidents of the community who end up identifying with the ones just mentioned or at least controlling them. There are also ministers of the word, who are not elected (maybe out of respect for a charism), while the presidents of the community indeed are elected. And the charism of those ministers of the word ends up being coordinated by the «inspectors and assistants» (the presbyterate?).

---

8 FAIVRE A., *Naissance d'une hiérarchie,* (Paris: Editions Beauchesne, 1977), 167.

Between structure and freedom (3rd Century)

The great advantage when we leave the 2nd century is that we not only find a great many more testimonies but also more *qualified* texts. We not only have writings «outside the subject» (that is, apologetic or narrative...) which refer to it only in passing, but also texts of a more «canonical» character which try to *order* ministerial *praxis* and regulate the life of the Church or texts which show the *observance* of that *praxis*, such as some of the letters of Saint Cyprian.

In relation to the first kind of texts, we have to recognize that a law does not reproduce life (many laws will be repeated precisely because they were not observed!), but at least they do reflect a way of thinking. And that way of thinking will gradually become more structuring and clerical.

The abundance of testimonies makes a summary exposition very difficult, since it cannot cover all of them. But in the same way that happens with the letters of Cyprian, we have a legal text that constitutes a privileged source. I am speaking of the *Traditio Apostolica* (TA) by Hippolytus.

The problems this brief work presents are not small. But it seems we can affirm that it dates from the first half of the 3rd century (perhaps *c.* 218), that there existed an earlier Egyptian version of the Latin version which we will comment on[9] and that almost certainly we can attribute this work to Hippolytus. There are also other versions of this work (Coptic, Syrian, Arab... and surely a Greek original which has been lost), which indicate its enormous diffusion among the churches of the 3rd century. This is also shown by the many documents derived from it (*Apostolic Constitutions, Epitome, Canon of Hippolytus...*).

On the other hand, the attribution to Hippolytus warns us, *a priori*, about the work's orientation. The author is a man renowned for his love of «order» and his strict guidance. He became the first antipope for his opposition to Pope Callistus on issues of disciplinary leniency related to penitence and marriage. It seems that he later abdicated, but maybe it was only martyrdom which freed him from becoming schismatic. In the prologue to the TA he considers the time has come to pass «from charity... to

---

9   That this Egyptian text, already known, was the TA, attributed to Hippolytus and considered to be lost, is the conclusion separately arrived at by E. Schwartz and R.H. Connolly. I follow here the introduction by B. Botte to the second edition of the TA in *Sources Chrétiennes* (1984).

tradition». And the work has three parts: one about the election and consecration of bishops and about the Eucharist; another about the faithful and about baptism (this thematic composition is itself significant). The third part is about various Christian customs.

According to what has been said, the information we can gather in the TA about the form of ministry in the 3rd century shows clearly a greater structuring and regulating zeal. In spite of everything, in the information in TA itself and elsewhere about life in the 3rd century there are sufficient signs that the increasing structuring still co-exists with ample margins of freedom. Hence we indicate the two parts of this section: control and freedom.

2.1.   ELEMENTS OF THE STRUCTURING OF MINISTRY

Even though it may seem very strange, there is no record anywhere of when and where the pastoral ministry broke up into «bishop» and «priest», moving away from the undifferentiated lexicon of the New Testament. If in the work of Ignatius of Antioch we already encountered that distinction, even though only as a *loose* testimony, now it seems to have become a *universal* fact. The ministry rests almost universally differentiated and established in a hierarchy of bishops, priests and deacons. And it is not only the TA which testifies to this.

In the same sudden way and with no easy explanation, the 3rd century testifies to a concentration of those ministries in relation to the *Eucharistic celebration* (what we can at this time call Christian «worship»).

That double concentration is reflected in two points we should note:

a) Language. In the first place it is reflected in an extremely important change in language: now it is these three offices —bishop, priest and deacon— which receive the name of *kleros* (the «portion of the Lord»), which is probably the word Tertullian translates as *ordo*[10] and gives rise to our present expression of «Sacrament of Holy *Orders*», the meaning of which is now so incomprehensible to the ordinary Christian.

The «delay of the parousia» seems to have had a lot to do with this change. When the end of time did not arrive, the believer also had to turn to «what is temporal». It seems then that «portion of the Lord» referred only to *those who dedicated themselves explicitly* to «things of the Lord» and not to their own

---

10 TERTULLIAN, *De exhortatione castitatis* 7,3 (Paris: Ed. Sources Chrétiennes, 1985), 92.

things. This implicit inference brings us very close again to the Old Testament situation or of «religious» in general[11]. And the notion of «clergy» (in its original sense) turns with this into something more «plausible» and more verifiable than that of «people of God».

In parallel we notice, too, —as I already mentioned— a sudden and very extensive appearance of the word *laity*, to designate those who do not belong to this triad of ministers. However (at least according to A. Faivre's explanation), the laity of the 3rd century still does not coincide with that of the 20th century: it does not have so much the meaning of *opposition* to the clergy as that of *nearness* to it. In truth, the appearance of the «clergy» has been something bad, as it is still *all* the faithful who should live as the clergy, that is, «for the Lord»[12]. This is why there are still some who will try to at least approach this impossible ideal and co-operate with it[13]. «Layman» is not here, then, he who is not «clergy», in the sense that he is *secular*, but he who still wants to be *people*, and in that way approaches being «portion of the Lord».

b) Imposition of hands. In addition to the change in language, we have, in what seems to happen with the laying on of hands, another expression of that concentration of the ministry which now acquires explicitly a double hierarchical meaning that it would be advisable to observe in more detail.

Let us explain that the concentration of functions will lead to one of these two things: 1) to having «remnants» sometimes of an absorbed function (that is, the «doctor» is absorbed by the «president» but there is a remnant which converts into the «reader»[14]); and 2) to the creation at times of auxiliary functions or lesser assistants when just one function cannot cover everything (in this way, for example, the «sub deacon» and probably the «acolyte», too, etc.). In both cases we have what later will be called «minor orders». But

---

[11] Even though not necessarily from a Christian perspective, as «the things of the Lord» are not strictly speaking those of worship, but those of the life of the brethren. That is why, in the text, I do not compare them to the things «of the earth» but to one's «own» things.

[12] That was the ideal for Clement of Alexandria, for Tertullian, etc., and Origen perceived it at a much more distant time. Cf. FAIVRE A., *Les laics aux origines de l'Église*, (Paris: Le Centurion, 1984), 160-161.

[13] Gradually, due to the inertia of «temporal things», that collaboration was to be reduced to assuring the material subsistence of the ministers of the Eucharist.

[14] Cf. FAIVRE A., *Naissance d'une hiérarchie*, (Paris: Editions Beauchesne, 1977), 67. It is not necessary to consider the enormous importance of the ministry of «reader» at a time when few knew how to read and in which *oral* transmission was almost the only source of contact with and transmission of the Word.

for now the structure is of *delegation downward*, more than of a plurality of charisms unified by the Spirit, as we were formulating when speaking of Paul.

So, in this state of things there is already a clear distinction in the rite of the imposition of the hands. The TA prescribes that hands should not be imposed if it is not in relation to the Eucharistic ministry (for example, on widows[15]). Opposite «ordination» now we find «installation». And it is not important if that installation is produced by the imposition of hands or not (as Hippolytus seems to prefer), since even in the first case it will be an imposition of hands *with a different meaning from that of the Eucharistic ministries.* This will bring about the distinction, even linguistic, between *cheirotonia* and *cheirothesia,* as we have already mentioned.

c) But this alone is not what is more important, but that both Hippolytus and Origen, or the *Didaskalia,* will justify this concentration and distinction… by resorting to an *Old Testament* typology! Presbyters and deacons are equated to the «priests» and «levites» of the Old Testament. Origen, more inclined to allegory, will use the image of the High Priest who went alone into the Holy of Holies[16]. We must add, however, that the recourse to the Old Testament nomenclature is, at least at the beginning, very elastic and imprecise. So, for example, the *Didaskalia* (II, 26, 2 and 3), at the same time that it admits that «only the bishops offer», adds immediately that «your priests are the deacons, the presbyters, the widows and the orphans». It is a pity that making the poor («widows and orphans») into priests, which would have compensated the clerical trajectory, did not impress itself in the history of the later Church.

Structuring, clericalization and priestly terminology were born together. Time will tell what of this is legitimate retrieval of Old Testament notions and what is *relapse* into the Old Testament (as we formulated in the first part). For the moment the plain fact is enough. Now we must examine the second of the stated elements.

But before that let us present a brief summary of this first part: the duality clergy-laity has appeared; the «clergy» has been assimilated into the Eucharist; the other ministries, so diverse before, are now only «remnants» or «secretariats»

---

15 Cf., TA, 10.

16 Cf. FAIVRE A., *Les laïcs aux origines de l'Église,* (Paris: Le Centurion, 1984), 130-131 and 94. The Old Testament typology is not completely innocent, as it implicitly bears the consequence of being able to «live off the altar».

(minor orders). Finally assimilation to the vocabulary of the Old Testament has been developing (high priest, priests, Levites...).

2. MARGINS OF FREEDOM

If on the points described above the 3rd century panorama anticipates today's reality, we must add that the information we have of that century differs also from our current situation thanks to the flexibility and the breathing space which that more structured reality still retained. It is convenient to briefly examine this flexibility since it can have an important *theological* meaning.

a) In relation to language. To begin with what is simpler, when Hippolytus presents his famous Eucharistic prayer, which largely coincides with the second Canon of our Mass, he deliberately warns that «it is not at all necessary that he (the bishop) prays with the very same words given above, as though by an effort of memory giving thanks (*eucharistein*) to God. Each shall pray whatever is according to his ability. If someone has the ability to pray a lengthy and solemn prayer, that is well. If someone else, in praying, offers a short prayer, this is not to be prevented. That prayer must only be correct in orthodoxy» (TA 9).

The Arab and Egyptian versions have suppressed this text or at least the particle *not*, so that they convert it to «absolutely necessary to repeat the same words». This bears witness to a situation several centuries later which approaches our present rigidity. But Hippolytus on the contrary is interested more in the *prayer* than in the *formula*; as long as formulas of monarchist or modalism inspiration are avoided (the allusion to «correct orthodoxy» seems to refer to this)[17].

b) In relation to ordination. More important still is that Hippolytus probably acknowledges the possibility that the Eucharist be presided over by non-ordained men, such as the «confessors» (or martyrs who had survived torture): the confessor «needs not hands laid upon him for the office of deacon or elder. He has the honor of the office of elder through his confession» (TA 9). Maybe here there is still beating a notion (lost nowadays) according to which ordination is not just the placing of power, but can also be recognition of a

---

17 Monarchism and modalism are two Trinitarian heresies discussed in those times, denying either the equality of Father, Son and Spirit, giving the supremacy to the Father, or the personal character of the divine «modes of existence».

06

Builders of Community

gift: there is a degree of «material» apostolicity or identification with Jesus which can replace even the total absence of formal apostolicity[18].

But it is also probable that the text of TA, identifying «presbyter» and «president» of the Eucharist, does not have the force we attribute to it today. Does Hippolytus suppose that identification? Or does he think that only the bishop is minister of the Eucharist? And in the second hypothesis, does he perceive him as the only minister *possible* or only as a *habitual* president (something that would not exclude other «extraordinary» presidents)? The text is not clear on this point. But it is convenient to note that the TA expressly adds: «If he (the confessor) is instituted as a bishop, then hands will be laid upon him» (TA 9). This difference makes total sense, even without considering the previous questions, and not only because the number of bishops is much more reduced and must be, accordingly, better controlled, but also because it allows the participation of the people in the election of the ultimate person responsible for each Church, something about which we will speak later on.

And this possible and surprising exception to the TA is not unique. In another famous text, Tertullian affirms that the need for ordination is only disciplinary, but that in themselves (and where no other thing is possible) cleric and layman are the same at the moment of the Eucharist:

«The laymen are they not all priests? It is written: «He made us a Kingdom of Priests to serve his God and Father» (Rev 1:6). It is the authority of the Church, and the honor which has acquired sanctity through the joint session of the Order, which has established the difference between the Order and the laity. Accordingly, where there is no joint session of the ecclesiastical Order, you offer, and baptize, and are priest, alone for yourself. But where three are, a church is, even if they are lay»[19].

18 The argument should also work the other way around. Years ago there was a famous movie (*Le Défroqué*) that pretended that an apostate and non-believer priest could consecrate the species simply because one day hands had been laid upon him and now he repeated mechanically some words (in Latin at that time): that *Renegade* was the opposite figure of the *Confessor* in the TA and it brings us again to the impossibility of a *mere* formal apostolicity. To put it in classical and safe terminology: the intention to «do as the Church does» would be missing, since the minimum intention of the Church is to follow Jesus. So, there was no real consecration of the species and the alleged dramatic force of *The Renegade* was rather melodramatic.

19 TERTULLIAN, *De exhortatione castitatis 7,3* (Paris: Ed. Sources Chrétiennes, 1985), 92. The second phrase says literally: «*differentiam inter ordinem et plebem constituit Ecclesiae auctoritas*», where «ordo» seems to translate the Greek *kleros*.

The force of this text lies in that its testimony is not intentional but indirect. Tertullian is not discussing clerics and laity, but second marriage. And he wants to prove that the prohibition of this affects also lay people (not accepted in the Church at that moment). That is why he tries to argue based on data accepted by all. He maintains: just as in the moment of the Eucharist you have (at least *de iure*) the same powers that the cleric has, so also in relation to monogamy you have the same obligations.

One could object that maybe it is a text of the Montanist not Catholic Tertullian. *De exhortatione castitatis* is dated between the years 204 and 212, and Tertullian became Montanist between 207 and 208. It is possible, then, that the work is Montanist. But it is not clear either if *a priori* one can say that the content is Montanist, independently of its date. As Montanism seems to be a mixture of rigorism, anarchism and charismatic elitism, it is not something easy to reconstruct by pure deduction. The force of Tertullian's text may lie in the fact that it is addressed *to all* (not only to the saints or charismatics) and it argues by quoting something known and accepted by his adversaries[20]. Accepting this text as valid, it would still be possible to continue maintaining the «essential difference» Trent spoke about between priest and layman: since it does not lie in the power of consecration (the whole Assembly consecrates) but, in the language of this book, in the fact that the president of the Eucharist be simply a member of the community or «man of the community».

And to complicate things even more, Firmilian, Bishop of Caesarea in Cappadocia, in a letter to Saint Cyprian provides a similar testimony, only this time it refers to a woman. It is about a lady who «presented herself as a prophetess and acted as if filled with the Holy Spirit», even though later it was discovered that she was an impostor with a dissolute life (who for example «deceived a priest, a countryman, and another, a deacon, so that they had intercourse with that same woman»). So, about this woman Firmilian tells us that «she frequently dared this: to pretend that with an invocation not to be condemned she sanctified bread and celebrated the Eucharist, and to offer sacrifice to the Lord, not without the

---

20 So accepted was it that still in the 11th century Abbot Guerrico wrote: «The priest does not consecrate alone, he does not offer alone, but all the community of the faithful consecrates and offers with him» (PL 85.87).

sacred recitation of the wonted formula; and also to baptize many, making use of the usual and lawful words of interrogation»[21].

The force —and the insufficiency— of this text seem to lie in that its author does not question at all the reference to the Eucharist. Firmilian is interested in the subject of baptism, which at that time opposed Cyprian to the Bishop of Rome, Esteban. The letter is a strong diatribe against the latter and against his rigor and severity towards Cyprian on this point. That is why Firmilian dispenses with the Eucharist and throws out immediately the question: can we really believe that the devil baptized through this woman, and that from that baptism followed the forgiveness of sins and the grace of the Trinity, considering that her formula was the correct one? Would Pope Esteban accept the validity of that baptism?[22].

In my opinion, the argument is not valid. Later theologians would perhaps have said that in that opportunistic woman the «intention of doing what the Church does» which, in baptism, expresses itself in the name of the Trinity, was missing, but in the ministry the intention of the Church lies in the continuity and in the «*sequela Iesu*». That is why the Pope could reject the baptisms of that woman and accept those of the heretics in which he did see that intention present[23]. But what is important for our theme is not this, but another question: could Firmilian present this testimony if the mere idea of a woman presiding at the Eucharist were totally unthinkable, because bizarre, in the Church at that time? If this were true, not being historical the anecdote

---

21 «*Ep.* 75,10» in CIPRIANO, *Obras*, (Madrid: BAC, 1964), 712-713. Something similar could also be stated in relation to the forgiveness of sins, a theme about which there are also some difficulties. Ignatius of Loyola says in his Autobiography that, before entering the battle in which he would be wounded, he made his confession to another soldier. The text does not reflect a mere particular superstition, but a certain ecclesial practice, as is shown by the recommendation of Lanfranc, Archbishop of Canterbury in the 11ᵗʰ century: «If you do not find a cleric *of whatever degree* to confess you, choose an honest man wherever you find yourself... A pure man can purify a guilty man in the absence of any clergy» (cited by COMBY J., *Para leer la historia de la Iglesia*, I, Estella: Verbo Divino, 1985, 153). Furthermore: in the personal diary Pope Pius II wrote during his pontificate, he relates very simply how King Henry of England, before one of the battles of the Hundred Years War, had exhorted his soldiers «to confess their sins between themselves» (*alter alteri peccata confiteamur*) to solicit God's help (cf. PIO II, *Commentarii rerum memorabilium quae temporibus suis contingerunt*, I, Ed. A. Van Heck, Cittá del Vaticano 1984, 385).

22 CIPRIANO, *Obras*, (Madrid: BAC, 1964), 714.

23 What we say here and in footnote 103 does not hamper the fact that there are other cases when that «intention of the Church» could be more complex and, so, more difficult to pinpoint with total precision (remember what was said in footnote 60, chap. 2). K. Rahner even says in relation to holy orders that the intention of the Church can be changeable, according to the times (cf. *Escritos de Teología*, VI, Taurus, Madrid 1969, 394). But even with these difficulties, this classic principle can become a good hermeneutic way for the solution of the extreme problems we have encountered.

used by Firmilian would not, with reason, be taken into account[24], so his argument would be left with no premise.

In this section we have brought together the texts which present more difficulties for the current situation. And even though they are too few to draw a conclusion as necessary, maybe they are sufficient to merit attention and study, as perhaps they open some possible paths. For now —and leaving everything unresolved since the data do not provide anything further— we move on to a third section, much more clear and compelling.

c) In relation to appointments. This third issue to be examined refers to the election of the ministers. Here, too, a balance is introduced into the structure we have presented. The intervention of the people in the bishop's election is, for Saint Cyprian, «divine tradition» and «apostolic practice»[25]. And this seems to be the reason why the TA decides that the confessor, whatever the merit of his martyrdom and even if to be a presbyter he does not need ordination, to be a bishop he does.

---

24 As would happen today if a bishop used the story that a woman who had officiated at Mass had deceived him or his clergy, In ancient times, on the contrary, data like in Rom 16:1-3 would give it weight, where Paul speaks of Phoebe who had been «president» of many (*prostatis*, a word with a certain technical character, even though it could also mean protectress); or Rom 16:7, which speaks about the couple Prisca and Aquila, companions in prison of Paul, who «are very considered among the *Apostles*». Also in the letter Pliny writes to Trajan, towards the year 112, asking about how to behave toward the Christians, he says: «I have considered it necessary to wrest the truth, even by torture, from two slaves with the title of *ministers*, but I was unable to discover something more than an irrational superstition...». These show that the problem of the ministry of women is not historically solved, even if it is not the theme for this book.

25 «For which reason you must diligently observe and keep the practice delivered from divine tradition and apostolic observance, which is also maintained among us, and almost throughout all the provinces; that for the proper celebration of ordinations all the neighboring bishops of the same province should assemble with that people for which a prelate is ordained. And the bishop should be chosen in the presence of the people, who have most fully known the life of each one, and have looked into the doings of each one as respects his habitual conduct...». The people should separate themselves from the sinning bishops «since they themselves have the power either of choosing worthy priests, or of rejecting unworthy ones». Because of this «we observe to come from divine authority, that the priest should be chosen in the presence of the people under the eyes of all, and should be approved worthy and suitable by public judgment and testimony» («*Ep.* 67,5:1; 3:2 and 4:1» in CIPRIANO, Obras, Madrid: BAC, 1964, 635 and 634). The same thing is affirmed by Cyprian about himself (*Ep.* 59, 6:1 in CIPRIANO, Obras, Madrid: BAC, 1964, 570) and of the Bishop of Rome, Cornelius, to refute in this way Novatian's claims: «was made bishop by the judgment of God and of His Christ, by the testimony of almost all the clergy, by the suffrage of the people who were then present, and by the assembly of ancient priests and good men» («*Ep.* 55,8:4» in CIPRIANO, *Obras*, Madrid: BAC, 1964. 526).

This is a fundamental principle for the early Church and, in reality, it derives from a broader ordination which affects not only the election of bishops but also the participation of the people and consultation of the latter in the Church's decisions[26]. This practice —in which Saint Cyprian was also model and example and which fits in with the procedure of the Apostles we observed in *Acts*— will become more difficult as time goes by. And not only due to the detail (accidental) that some «confessors» took advantage of it and of the respect the community had for them to make the governance of his church almost impossible for Cyprian[27], but (more structurally) because as the Church became more aware of its universality («catholicity»), many decisions affecting a church are taken *away* from each local community (in interdiocesan synods, etc.), so that they cannot be easily consulted. But the principle remains and Cyprian tries at least to lessen the difficulties by giving detailed and accomplished information to his people[28].

And this broader principle of the people's participation is correlative to another which also has roots in the New Testament: the autonomous configuration of the different local churches. According to the theology underlying this principle, each local church is, in some way, the whole *ekklesía*, except in what has to do with the bishop, who has a *wider* responsibility and as a consequence can be a uniting factor (not only of his community, but) *between the different local churches*. The bishop is not only *for* the local church nor is he only *of* the local church. Here is an intimation of a germinal collegiality which is manifested in the bishop's consecration ceremony: even though the community participates in his *election*, however the *ordination* is not in the hands of the community but in the hands of the bishops of the

---

26 «From the beginning of my episcopate I determined not to make any resolution on my own, without your counsel and the *consent of my people*» («*Ep.* 14, 1» in CIPRIANO, *Obras*, Madrid: BAC, 1964. 412). The reasons for this behavior are employed also by the Bishop of Carthage: «It would be wearisome for me and very badly viewed if I took decisions alone… (that affect many) and what did not count with *the assent of many* could not have considerable strength» («*Ep.* 30, 6» in CIPRIANO, *Obras*, Madrid: BAC, 1964, 452). Or: «About this issue I do not think that I pass judgment on my own as still many of the clergy are missing… and the case of each should be studied and weighed in all detail, not only with my colleagues, but *with the whole people*. As what can create a precedent for the future should be studied with moderation and equilibrium…» («*Ep.* 34, 1» in CIPRIANO, *Obras*, Madrid: BAC, 1964, 467-468; underlined by me).

27 There are temperaments for which it is easier to be heroes for a moment or *brief* time than to be patient or respectful over a *long* period. Life shows this in a thousand ways.

28 This is why several of his letters are addressed to «the presbyters, deacons and people».

neighboring churches. On this issue, Cyprian and the TA coincide with the Church of Rome.

d) In relation to creativity. Where there is more autonomy there is usually more creativity and this is the last point to illustrate.

The zeal for structure and control during this century did not reach the extreme of totally extinguishing the fact —we already found in the New Testament— that the ministries which sprang up were often linked to concrete historical needs. According to the *Didaskalia* of Syria, the existence of deaconesses seems to have had to do with very practical requirements, like not scandalizing pagans (in visits to women) or preventing possible acts against modesty in baptismal immersions:

«Wherefore, O bishop, appoint thee workers of righteousness as helpers who may cooperate with thee unto salvation. Those that please thee out of all the people thou shalt choose and appoint as deacons: a man for the performance of the most things that are required, but a woman for the ministry of women. For there are houses whither thou canst not send a deacon to the women, on account of the heathen, but may send a deaconess. Also, because in many other matters the office of a woman deacon is required. In the first place, when women go down into the water, those who go down into the water ought to be anointed by a deaconess with the oil of anointing; and where there is no woman at hand, and especially no deaconess, he who baptizes must of necessity anoint her who is being baptized. But where there is a woman, and especially a deaconess, it is not fitting that women should be seen by men: but with the imposition of hand do thou anoint the head only. As of old the priests and kings were anointed in Israel, do thou in like manner, with the imposition of hand, anoint the head of those who receive baptism, whether of men or of women; and afterwards —whether thou thyself baptize, or thou command the deacons or presbyters to baptize— let a woman deacon, as we have already said, anoint the women. But let a man pronounce over them the invocation of the divine Names in the water. And when she who is being baptized has come up from the water, let the deaconess receive her, and teach and instruct her how the seal of baptism ought to be (kept) unbroken in purity and holiness»[29].

29 *Didaskalia Apostolorum* III, 12: 1-3. What is striking in this work is the concern about the sexual morality of the clergy, to the point that sometimes it seems that the author sees in this the difference between clergy and laity (even though he accepts a married bishop: cf. II, 2: 1-2). Even though he urges the bishop above all to be merciful as is God with sinners, threatening him if he makes his own virtue into a motive to deny pardon and mercy to others.

In short: the evolution in this 3rd century leaves some margins for creativity in the possibility of presidents of the Eucharist without holy orders, in the appointment of bishops by election[30] and in certain liturgical and ministerial creativity.

2.3. READINGS FROM HISTORY

All this somewhat formless gathering of data suggests some important points for theological reflection which we will reduce to three key sections.

2.3.1. NECESSARY STRUCTURING

We will see later on how all this process of structuring is accompanied by great dangers. This does not mean at all that they are not necessary and that they do not come in part imposed by the very nature of things. Human history is like this and there are in it few necessary things which are not *at the same time* dangerous (only the buried and barren talent is devoid of risk). Sometimes this gives rise in history to wild steps being taken and progressing without taking the risks into account (until they end up paying the price, instead of reaching the goal); and at other times it gives rise to unbelieving conservatisms which become paralyzed in order to avoid risks (until they end up preserving fossils and losing the life they endeavored to keep).

This consideration, so obvious, has much to do with our theme. It would be naïve to think that a church which lives pressed by persecutions and heresies (which in these first centuries were much more than mere theoretical discussions and threatened to disintegrate the community) would not feel the need to group together and have an axis around which it can focus[31]. This is what the

---

30 On this so important issue see my book: «*Ningún obispo impuesto*» (*S. Celestino 1*). *Las elecciones episcopales en la historia de la Iglesia*. Santander: Sal Terrae, 1992.

31 Suffice to think about the great confusion produced in the Church by the problem of the reconciliation of schismatics or the issue of the *lapsi* (apostates during the persecution of Decius) which was one of the crosses of Saint Cyprian and one of the motives of the schism of Felicissimo. The people —with an understandable reaction of self-defense, but not very Christian— persisted in not forgiving the apostates. Cyprian and many other bishops advocated reconciliation with penance, but they wanted to convince the people and not impose it on their own, as was expressed in footnote 111. In this context Cyprian on more than one occasion laments «if you could participate with me, my dear brother, when these deviants return from the schism, you would see how much it costs me to convince our brothers to have patience and to calm their indignation so they consent to receive and remedy the guilty ones» («*Ep.* 59, 15:3» in CIPRIANO, *Obras*, Madrid: BAC, 1964, 581). Cyprian would even accept that on some occasions he was the mistaken one and that those schismatics did not return repentant to the church... So, in this context, a series of imprudent «confessors», for a desire of prominence or for vanity, assigned

bishops end up being more and more, which can explain theologically the appearance of the monarchical episcopate, independently of how we explain it historically.

To all this, too, were added a series of practical demands. For example: the churches kept growing in number and assets and the bishop gradually became a *trustworthy* administrator of the assets of the Christian community. The whole development which begins here can, at another time, present contradictions which it will be advisable to correct. But one cannot present all the progressive institutionalization of the ecclesial ministry as simple apostasy vis-à-vis alleged so-called «evangelical spontaneity» of its origins, since this would be equivalent to confusing the Church with the child in *The Tin Drum* by Günter Grass, who refused to believe because he did not want to pay the price. I repeat: this in no way means that growing up does not have its risks which one should endeavor to avoid and correct.

Historically speaking I believe to be accurate the following assessment by J. Rius:

«Between the most archaic and primitive Documents and the later ones, one can observe a significant evolution with respect to the proliferation, stratification and specialization of the different ministries, both masculine and feminine. But at the same time as this evolution is taking place, one can observe another one no less interesting: there is a process of progressive imitation, first of the Jewish communities, in relation to the organization of the community in its various functions and celebrations, to end later on in an iron-clad organization based on stereotypes in which the role has given way to the title and the celebration of the cultic ritual. This phenomenon observed in the present sample of writings that belong in some way to the Syrian Hellenistic area should be studied with care and on a greater scale, expanding to other similar writings»[32].

But at the same time it is a theologically expected assessment. And without going into the expansion the author proposes, one could anticipate that the results will be very similar to what he has found in the Syrian Hellenistic sphere,

to themselves the power of intercession or reconciliation without any penitence. How could such a community not disintegrate in such a situation (so «probable» from a human point of view), without a minimum of structure of control and authority?

All this is undeniable, even though one could add that not all epochs are times of persecution in the history of the Church.

[32] ASOCIACIÓN JUAN XXIII, *Teología y Magisterio*, Salamanca: Sígueme, 1987, 110. (The chapter of J. Rius is entitled «Diversificaciones de ministerios en el área sirohelenista: de Ignacio de Antioquia a las Constituciones Apostólicas», 75-113).

in its successes and in its risks. Only that this in no way means that such evolution should be canonized by us as the norm for today in all its aspects. It means simply that the mission of the theologian, when dialoguing with history, is not to condemn or canonize history, but to learn from it to sort out the present.

That is why, once the need for this evolution has been established, we are going to try to learn from its successes and its contradictions.

2.3.2. *PRESERVING COLLEGIALITY*

The most significant aspect of the structuring of the ministry into bishops-priests-deacons is probably the collegiate character of the presbyterate (which in turn is a reflection of the collegiate character of the episcopate). This fact remains unchanged from the time of the early community in Jerusalem and enables us to establish an important theological principle: the Church is collegial and, seen *ad intra*, the structure of the ministry is also collegial. The ecclesiastical ministry has an *ad extra* dimension which makes it collegial and a dimension *ad intra* which makes it «collegial» in a community. As Karl Rahner writes:

> «And in point of fact the New Testament and the primitive Church do not actually show any knowledge of the single priest but only of the presbyterium. (...) Therefore if the "second grade" of the priestly office is really to be *iuris divini*, it can only be thought of as the college for the bishop; strictly speaking, therefore, priests do not primarily take the place of the bishop where he cannot be himself, but support him as the presbyterium surrounding the bishop where he is»[33].

This fact must co-exist with other facts, but cannot be wiped out by them. And neither the necessary head of any college nor the great difficulty in the practical realization of the collegial in many numerous colleges can make it disappear, because what the Church received from Jesus was precisely, and only, a collegial ministry: the apostolic college. The Pope and the bishop are, of course, heads of their respective colleges, but neither can exert their position as head reducing the college to a sort of «minor orders», because then they would not be heads, but *the whole* organism. It is something that nowadays seems to happen more frequently than is advisable.

---

33 RAHNER K., «The Bishop In The Church», in *Theological Investigations*, VI, Darton Longman & Tood, London, 1974, 341.

And, curiously, a factor which seems to have influenced this negative situation will be the later ontological «priestliness» of the ministry we condemned in the first part of this work. So, when this happened the ministry started to be considered more and more *in itself and by itself*, independently of its integration as a college which is constitutive of ministry, precisely as «person of the community», which is structured as «community of communities».

And this last observation brings us to reflect on another of the facts that were highlighted in the 3rd century: the almost total absorption and concentration of the ministries in the Eucharistic celebration.

2.3.3. EUCHARIST AND AUTHORITY

At the start of section 2.1 we were saying that it is not easy to explain how that concentration of the ministries around the Eucharist came about. The argument that at the Last Supper only the Apostles were present and that consequently only to them is entrusted the commission of the Lord is exegetically very forced. But now we would like to show that, even though difficult to explain for the historian, this phenomenon is possible to understand for the theologian. The Church keenly perceived there should be a necessary harmony between «presiding over the Eucharist» and «presiding over the community» (and maybe more so in times of persecution or difficulty). Because *authority in the Church should always be as the presidency in the Euchari*st: a way of keeping present and alive the memory of the selfless life of Jesus, so that this remembrance creates communion; a presidency which is not «private property», so that the president could «deny communion» to those who «are not of his line» or do not commune *with him* (as if communion with him were equivalent to communion *with Christ*). In this way, the Eucharist symbolically anticipates the conversion of worldly authority into evangelical authority. This is why the approximation or identification between the president of the community and the president of the Eucharist is both coherent and expressive: «the Eucharist makes the Church and the Church makes the Eucharist» (De Lubac).

But all this, which seems undeniable, has its dangers. And these dangers will begin to be realized as the Eucharist starts to be seen not from the *ephapax* of Jesus (Heb 9:12), which leads necessarily to the mission and to the Church being missionary, but as perfectly univocal with the religious category of «worship», which can completely dispense with mission. Then the presidency of the Eucharist will not serve to correct evangelically the presidency of the community,

but arbitrarily divinize authority from the religious notion of what is «priestly»[34].
Then, as A. Faivre writes correctly, the faithful will go «from belonging to the
people *of* priests to being people of *the priests*»[35].

That today we are more or less in this situation I think is true. Here we see
manifested what we have called before «counter-signs» of all the historical development which have to be corrected with the passing of time. But this observation takes us out of the 3rd century. We wonder if all of this does not produce a
gradual misrepresentation of «ordination». It seems that at the beginning the
imposition of hands was necessary for *entrusting the mission of unifier of a community which, in itself, is also missionary* (this we saw in our assessment of the New
Testament). But with the rapprochement between this task and the Eucharistic
presidency (plus the need to control the Eucharist which we saw speaking of
Ignatius of Antioch), *an almost total displacement of the ordination from the apostolate to the Eucharist* seems to take place (even with the presidency of the community in the «Pastorals»). And all this makes way for the idea of the transmission
of a «cultic or sacred power».

But then, this sacred power will become the *only basis* for authority, which,
previously, was partly rooted in the people's acceptance, which was a necessary
condition for ordination. This hypothetical change in the meaning of ordination is another of those issues that should be studied in more detail. This would
imply a recovery of the missionary aspect of the Eucharist («we announce»…
«we proclaim»…). Because, if the Eucharist were not missionary, it could not
constitute the Church, nor could it be constituted by it.

We have focused extensively on this century because probably it is the most
important in the whole evolution of the ministry. Subsequent centuries only
bring consolidations and further details of this fundamental movement.

---

34 In the language of today's experience one could say it is the emergence of «grumpy priests»; now
one cannot even ask ministers to behave toward the people outside the Eucharist as he behaves
in it, because there are some who even within the Eucharist do not behave well toward others.

35 «*Ainsi les laïcs, appartenant au peuple des prêtres, deviendront-ils très vites, le peuple des prêtres*».
(FAIVRE A., *Les laïcs aux origines de l'Église*, Le Centurion, Paris 1984, 94). It is a very expressive
word play which loses its power in translation.

Justification and organization in the 4ᵗʰ century

∽

The 4ᵗʰ century does not provide information of great interest, as it has a certain character of continuity, but also novelty, in relation to the 3ʳᵈ century. The continuity stems from the very dynamic of the evolution begun in the previous century. The novelty stems from the new and peaceful relationship between the Church and the Empire, a relationship initiated by Constantine and which created a situation of:

a) *liberty*, so incredible, so longed for and so newly-arrived that it is idealized as if it signified the coming of the Kingdom[36];

b) *extension*, derived from the almost forced increase of conversions, but with the consequence of a progressive degradation in the levels of «*sequela Iesu*» of the Church[37];

c) *a new type of conflict with the authorities* and, concretely, with the emperors. Now the authorities are not external persecutors but sympathizers, protectors and even members of the Church. But this will not avoid tension.

These newly-formed factors not only create new problems, but also condition the evolution of the old ones. All in all, we can say that in reference to our theme of ecclesial ministry this evolution points clearly to a double goal: *structuring*, on the one hand, and theological *justification* on the other, of the new situation which has emerged.

We will first examine these two aspects of the continuing line and then very briefly we will examine some of the new problems connected with ecclesial ministry in the relationship with the Empire.

3.1. SYSTEMATIZATION OF THE PREVIOUS SITUATION

What I would most like to highlight about this systematization —to link with things already mentioned— is not so much its content but how it can end up having, in the long run, highly questionable consequences, even though in itself it

---

36 Reading texts of that time one cannot help comparing with some things seen and heard in 1979, after the triumph of the Sandinista Revolution in Nicaragua, or after any other of the victorious moments in human history which always engender exhorbitant hopes about the future.

37 For example, writings of that time testify that many people would put off baptism so as not to live with such a serious commitment. And that, among the Christians, «*sine, nondum est baptizatus*» (leave him be, he is still not baptized) worked as an excuse for less moral conduct…

is perfectly understandable and even praiseworthy. I will formulate it saying that *a logical thirst for sanctity and for experience, and the urgency to avoid abuses will create the basis for a structuring of the ministry as «separation», as «career» and as «control».* We will examine these three issues.

3.1.1. THIRST FOR HOLINESS

Once the ministry was localized in that concentrated triad around the altar, it is logical to think that the Church would be concerned about the sanctity of the life of those in the «holy of holies». Because, even though the Eucharist starts tending toward the cultic, the Church is certainly still aware that God's sanctity is not in rites but in living.

To this one should add a pair of factors which perhaps influenced even more this zeal for sanctity. The first is the practice of *pardon*. It is believed (since the impact produced by the martyrs) that it is through the saints that God forgives the rest of us. And pardon is bestowed by the ministers of the altar, because the reconciliation of the community is expressed and realized through the Eucharistic communion. Does this not demand the sanctity of those who bestow pardon?

The second factor is, again, *the problem of the confessors*, whose sanctity (derived from their testimony as martyrs even if they did not die) gave them great internal authority before the people. We already noted how some abused this authority in the matter of the *lapsi*. Now that there are no more persecutions, those who are left tend to abuse much more. So sometimes they allow themselves to recommend or even reconcile on their own, etc. We have also seen that this presented problems for the leaders of the communities. Now we can add that it forced them, at the same time, «to not be less saintly».

As an example, as a consequence of this zeal, there was to be a gradual rapprochement between the ministers and monks (who came about as a protest against the worldliness of the Church and seeking a substitute for martyrdom). Who can devote himself to the Church and be a man of the community better than he who has decided to consecrate himself to a radically evangelical life? Is not all the reason for being Church in the gospel?

And this rapprochement was to lead to the imposition of sexual abstinence, in view of the fact that the men of the community cannot retire into the desert. An imposition which is more lenient in the East and stronger in the West (even though in the West there is of course «laicization» or «secularization» for those who do not comply), but which rests on the same principle of drawing closer to the monks and, through them, to the martyrs or confessors.

Only that this abstinence, in the long run, will set up a barrier separating the ecclesial ministry and the people (note this for later on). A barrier which does not derive so much from how celibacy can «brand» the psychology of *the person*, as from the undeniable fact that it creates such *states of things* that it is not easy to go from one to the other (for instance because of family responsibilities and because maybe celibacy can be imposed upon a chosen minister, but it could not be imposed on his wife if he is married)[38].

So the understandable zeal for sanctity will contribute in the long run, and largely unexpectedly, to a configuration of the ministry *as a group separated from the people.* Without wishing it, chastity leads to a caste system, unless this situation is compensated in some other way.

3.1.2. THIRST FOR EXPERIENCE

Those who wanted to become clerics were also made, prior to this, to go through all the tasks in the community. This eagerness is understandable not only to give example but also to gain experience. So, for example, Nicaea would legislate that a neophyte cannot be ordained bishop, reaffirming in this way the line of thought we already found in the «Pastoral Letters».

But in the long run —and against any prediction— this would lead to a devaluation of the tasks themselves, seeing them simply as phases on the way. An evolution will begin in this way which will turn those tasks into steps on a promotion ladder: from being *services* they will become *stages.* And this in turn will originate in protocol sensibilities, of which canon 18 of Nicaea is a good testimony: the deacon should not impart communion to the priest, nor place himself nearer the bishop, nor touch the species when the priest is present. Underneath this regulation it is easy to predict latent grudges about dignity. The reason given shows very clearly that the deacon «does not have the power to offer» and so is «inferior» to the priest, in spite of his strong link to the bishop: «*scientes quod episcoporum ministri sunt, presbyteris autem inferiores probentur*»[39].

---

[38] This, nonetheless, was attempted, for example in Spain and in the Council of Nicaea, where, according to the historian Socrates, only the intervention of the Bishop of Alta Tebaida, Pafnucio —who was celibate and renowned for his sanctity— stopped it from becoming law (cf. Socrates, *Historia Eclesiástica* I,II. PG. 67

[39] Cf. ALBERIGO G., *Conciliorum oecumenicorum decreta*, (Freiburg: Herder, 1962), 13-14. Permit me two observations about this decree:

I speak of «need» because precisely the new situation of the Church gave rise to certain civil privileges for ecclesial functions (i.e. on the subject of taxes, etc.) This will soon lead to an increase in these functions (in practical terms of the «minor» ones: lector, etc.), with the resulting need for control in order to avoid «profiteers».

Time will witness the coming of:

a) a more rigid and fixed structure which does not allow the free creation of functions according to need; and not only the «creation» but also the transfer of functions from one place to another[40]. This principle —applicable to any of the three functions— ended up being so severe that after Nicaea Gregory of Nazianzus was forced to leave the See of Constantinople because he had previously been bishop of another city. In the end (as could be expected) it was not carried out. But today, on the contrary, there are bishops who «climb» due to excessive mobility; in this way there is awakened an eagerness for «a career» of which we find today sad examples in some dignitaries.

b) A ceremony of «installation» much more controlled, ritualized and mandatory, now with an imposition of hands, too, —not «ordination»— even for the «minor» functions, which will in time justify their being called «orders», too.

c) And, with understandable logic, an extension of the word «clergy» to these minor functions or «orders». This is reflected in Canon 19 of Nicaea, according to which the deaconesses «should be counted totally *among the lay*, given they *do not have* any sort of imposition of hands».

a) One should notice the clarity with which it is established that the priest has the «*potestas offerendi*» and the deacon does not; precisely the situation nowadays. If historians show that this situation can be dated already to the previous century, then the text about the automatic incorporation of «confessors» to the presbyterate, which we quoted before with certain reservations, would acquire total value.

b) We can guess a sort of equation of the deacon to what today would be «private secretary» of the bishop. This would occasion, on the part of deacons, the classical presumption of all secretaries because they have more personal access to the bishop and greater possibilities of persuasion, etc., etc.

40 Canon 16 of Nicaea tries to prevent priests from changing from a particular church to another on their own or that those a bishop did not wish to ordain go to another for ordination. One can see a certain reason in not accepting so-called «absolute ordination» (without a church in which to serve), more than a century before canon 6 of Chalcedon which prohibited it (Schilllebeeckx attaches great importance to this in his book). However, the problem of «absolute ordinations» is not yet resolved in a clear way which can integrate sufficiently the difficult duality of local and universal facets. Many members of the Roman Curia are ordained bishops «of no church» only so they can feel strong enough to oppose or direct local bishops. All of this is profoundly contrary to the life and tradition of the Church.

So it is that a perfectly comprehensible zeal desiring more sanctity, more experience and less personal gain opens the door to an evolution that will shape the ecclesial ministry as a system of separation from the people, a system of career and personal advancement and rigid control. In a somewhat forced play of words, chastity led to caste, path to career and severity to rigidity. The intentions were excellent, but the complexity of the life of human beings plays tricks sometimes. And this is not the only problem for, once separated from the initial good intentions a situation like this must have recourse to some theoretical justification to maintain itself.

3.2. **JUSTIFICATION FOR THIS DEVELOPMENT**

This justification theory will not appeal merely to the Old Testament, as we saw happening in the 3rd century. Now, with the Church's full inculturation into Platonism, it can make use of a metaphysics of being as «hierarchy», whose best-known representative is «Pseudo-Dionysius». The sequence of titles in his work according to which to a *Heavenly Hierarchy* follows another work called *Ecclesiastical Hierarchy*, is eoloquent. And his thesis is clear: the hierarchy of the Church reflects the hierarchy of beings: «ours is a Hierarchy of the inspired and Divine and Deifying science»[41].

In a Plotinian vision of reality, everything is ordered by its distance in relation to God. This distance decides its sanctity and dignity until reaching matter which is what is most distant from God and also what is more worthless or bad. According to this, for our author, «each rank of those about God is more god-like than that which stands further away»[42]. The «higher» degrees are «at once more luminous, and more illuminating». This is why «the blessed *Tearchia* (the power of God) bequeathed, by Divine Goodness, the Hierarchy, for preservation, and deification of all rational and intellectual beings»[43].

Hierarchy is, practically, what gives content to the divine image and likeness of the human being. The whole New Testament theme of the *kenosis* of God has disappeared here: the revealed God in Jesus has been substituted by the god of Plato. And the metaphor of the body is substituted by the metaphor of the ladder[44].

---

41 *De ecclesiastica hierarchia* I, I (PG 3, 369).

42 «VIII *Ep*».: PG 3, 1092 B. Quoted from FAIVRE A., *Naissance d'une hiérarchie*, (Paris: Editions Beauchesne, 1977), 179.

43 *De ecclesiastica hierarchia* I, IV (PG 3, 376 B).

44 The great orthodox theologian J. Meyendorff believes that even though Pseudo-Dionysius «mentions without doubt the name of Jesus Christ and confesses his faith in the incarnation...

To find *this character of the being reflected in the very structure of the Church*, Pseudo-Dionysius considers as «priestly» or clerical *all* the ecclesial functions, from the episcopal down to the last of the minor orders. This is why he establishes the imposition of hands for all of them, without distinguishing too much between what are to be called *cheirotonía* and *cheirothesía*, to which we have already referred[45]. He distinguishes between the different orders, adding a quantity of symbolic rites for the ordination of each one, but in such a way that the superior order in addition to its particular rite has to pass through all the inferior rites… This hierarchical scale of the ordination rites reproduces ecclesial life, where, as we already mentioned, one must go through all the orders, one after the other, starting from the most inferior. As Faivre comments accurately, «to the absorption of the different functions corresponds the absorption of the rites of ordination. Parallelism is perfect and the hierarchical mechanism is exercised in all domains»[46].

What is questionable about this vision of Pseudo-Dionysius is highlighted in the indisputable conclusion he derives from his system: if things are like this, it follows that an unworthy, unholy minister will automatically be excluded from the rank of his order, which in turn implies the nullity of the administered sacraments. As is well known, the Church rejected Pseudo-Dionysius' conclusion which should imply the rejection of the precedent. However, this remains as tacit or environmentally assumed or, at least, not questioned.

In this way, to the three features we used to characterize this century (*separation, promotion ladder, and control*) a fourth is now added which justifies them intellectually: *sacralization*. And this sacralization will end up entailing the impossibility of critique: since if in principle they are saints, critique turns into blasphemy. A principle which still survives and would reach its culmination when Gregory XVI indignantly rejects the patristic idea of the church «*semper reformanda*» appealing to the Church's holiness.

the structure of his system has total independence in relation to his profession of faith». (*Christ in Eastern Christian Thought*, Washington: Corpus, 1969), 81. I am afraid that disassociation is still alive in many Catholic mentalities.

45 What is important to Pseudo-Dionysius in the subject of the imposition of hands is not the *transmission of the mission*, but the fact that it expresses the *submission to God*. «This rite shows the protection of God… and teaches to discharge all the priestly functions as under God, considering Him as Superior in all the acts of life» (*De ecclesiastica hierarchia* V, III, 263[PG 3, 512 A]).

46 FAIVRE A., *Naissance d'une hiérarchie*, (Paris: Editions Beauchesne, 1977), 178.

With all this we are, practically, at the current state of things: *hier*-archia has been born (*sacred* power) as opposed to laity (or *secular* being). Subsequent centuries would do no more than small tinkering with this structure. For example —as we will now see— political struggles and lack of culture will many times convert the lay man not into a simple non-sacred *power* but into the *poli-archia*, that is: the political power, or a man with a non-sacred power. Many of the aberrations of the theory of «the two spades» of Boniface VIII seem less aberrant from this view. But it is obvious, too, how the internal shaping of the Church resounds in the external way in which it is presented to the world.

3.3.   NEW PROBLEMS FOR THE MINISTRY AND THE LAITY

We saw in the biblical section how naturally the infant Church had assumed and almost copied the structure of the Jewish community. If we had more room we could equally show how naturally the Church «liberated» by Constantine would take on the Empire's political, economic and administrative model. The bishop coincides with the figure of the chief of a citizens' community. To the integration of the cities in a province will correspond then the appearance of a metropolian, with a more important role for the bishop of the metropolitan capital as he will be the one to convene a provincial council and preside (or confirm) the ordination of the bishops in the province, as is stated in Canon 4 of Nicaea. From Diocletian onwards, the provinces were grouped into large territories called «dioceses» and some of the great Patriarchs will be among the bishops of these diocesan capitals (Antioch, Alexandria, etc.).

This brief survey only aims to show, again, how the Church is not structured «from heaven» but from an interaction between the historical situation and the configuration of the Church, without detriment to the latter trying to be «alternative» community in many areas (for example, through the democratic election of the bishops in a world of imperial structure; or through the presbyteral ordination of slaves or the recognition of marriage between a liberator and a freed person, something which the Empire did not recognize as legitimate, etc., etc.). Anyway, perhaps of more importance for our reflection is the concrete issue of the relationship with the Emperor. As strange as it may seem today it is very clear that, at the beginning, the figure of Emperor «liberator of the Church» was equated to an ecclesial ministry. Constantine was named «bishop of those outside» and «thirteenth apostle» even before being baptized… This was easier as the emperors continued using the pagan title of «*pontifex maximus*» and the bishops had appropriated the Jewish title of «*summus pontifex*». But this linguistic mirage will give place to a brutal Caesero-papism which will force the Church to moderate its enthusiasm and react against it.

It is not a question of detailing the history of this reaction and all the conflicts it provoked, the best known of which is the one of Theodosius with St. Ambrose. Suffice to note that towards the year 375 the Emperor Gratian would resign the title of Pontifex Maximus. This separation will be much clearer in the West; in the East the Caesero-papism will continue along with the intervention of the emperors, in the course of the 5th century, in the convocation of the great councils, even though a 4th century emperor (Valentinian) had already learned to answer one of the Eastern Bishops who asked for the convocation of a council: «I am a *lay* person and I should not deal with those things»[47]. Despite this, in the 5th century (and in the West) Pope St. Leo, following a positive experience with the Emperor in relation to the imposition of the Council of Chalcedon, would still attribute to the Emperor the «inspiration of the Holy Spirit»[48].

But in spite of the practical inconsistencies, these skirmishes would serve to establish the aforementioned «conceptual precision»: now the term «lay» will be applied preferably not to the simple faithful but to the politically powerful (the emperor and later on to the feudal lord or the king...). This tacit shift in the meaning would go on practically until Philip IV of France[49]. But in this curious form of distinguishing (clergy ≈ sacred power; laity ≈ political power) is already in germ the whole of the subsequent development: Caeasero-papism in the East as well as the investiture controversy in the West. In one, due to identification with *power*; in the other, because of the struggle for *power*.

---

47 FAIVRE A., *Les laïcs aux origines de l'Église*, (Paris: Le Centurion, 1984), 171.
48 About this issue see GRILLMEIER A., *Jesus der Christus im Glauben der Kirche*, II, (Freiburg-Basel-Wien: Herder, 1986), 164-165; also the article of VOIGT K. quoted there about the «infallibility» of the Emperor.
49 As I already implied this makes more comprehensible the language of the bull *Clericis laicos* (by Boniface VIII in 1296) and of the document in response (*Antequam essent clerici*) to the theologians of the French king. In the former, and with the superior attitude which characterized him, the Pope writes «that the laity is enemy of the clergy is highly evidenced by antiquity and is shown clearly by today's experience». How far are we from what was lived in the early centuries of the Church! And how much this mentality of Boniface VIII survives still in a good portion of the clergy!

Justified in the 4th century, the evolution begun in the 3rd century was to continue during the 5th century. And also it will intensify thanks to the new and difficult circumstances that arise in that century. With this will diminish, too, the compensatory elements of that evolution we had seen in the 3rd century (cf. section 2.2, chapter 3).

These new circumstances are well known: the fall of the Western Empire and the subsequent crisis in society. The fall of Rome is —in the negative sense— a factor as astonishing and unthinkable as had been —in the positive sense— the conversion of the Empire in the previous century. The writings at the time reflect this. But it would not affect our subject if it were not for the fact that the tremendous crisis in that society —and in a Church less strong-willed than the one of the persecutions— great difficulties in the recruiting and preservation of the ecclesial ministers will emerge. This contributes to the relaxation of discipline and one can see how the Popes Innocent I (401-417) and Zosimus, his successor, insist on maintaining the organizational structures: people married for the second time or those who have been soldiers cannot be accepted… nor those who have not spent sufficient time in the «minor» functions until deserving of the «reward» of the «eminent dignity of presbyterate»[50].

One can guess the good will of these intentions, but it is easy also to perceive their insufficiency and their contra-indications, as we will see.

4.1. INCREASE IN NEGATIVE EFFECTS

4.1.1. *CAREER*

To start with, the inevitable shortening of the time of permanence in them, as a way of gaining more priests, contributes even more to shaping the diverse ministries as a «career» in which the «minor» services are merely *steps*. This is reinforced by the fact that some of them are kept on even after having lost their function with the passing of time, so that they were reduced to mere waiting rungs. How far we are from what had been the plurality of the ministries in the Churches of Paul!

---

50 Cf. FAIVRE A., *Naissance d'une hiérarchie*, (Paris: Editions Beauchesne, 1977), 321-328.

A small example in our days, because it is only its ultimate logical conse-quence, can help us understand precisely how aberrant this evolution was. I refer to the «privilege» —in which I also participated— given to the Jesuits in order to «not comply with the interstices» prescribed in passing from one order to another: «the minor orders» were all received on the same day, and the three «major» ones (sub-deacon, deacon and priest) on three successive days. *In itself* it is a reasonable subterfuge from a practical point of view (why tarry in purely nominal realities?…). But the theological vision supporting this is deplorable because it involves an acceptance that the majority of the ministries are, in themselves, nothing. Each one of them is a mere «step» for the next one.

And, without going to such extremes, one can see easily, by the turn taken in this century, how what in the 4th century was meant to be an *experience require-ment* has become mechanical elevation or *pure reward*. This is why it will not be strange that Popes of that century, like Celestine and St. Leo, end up equating ecclesial ministry to the military career. The ministry is the «*militia divina*» and the way through the different steps is justified by appealing to what happens… in the army[51].

4.1.2. *STATUS, MORE THAN A ROLE*

Having stopped being «function» (or becoming something purely nominal) it is practically impossible for the *exercise* of a public ministry constitute anyone a member of the «clergy» (within the wider sense of the word we already found in the 4th century). This is why between this century and the next the need was gradually felt to *convert some into clergy* (something inconceivable in days gone by, since for that *real* tasks and missions were entrusted). And this is why the «tonsure» appears as a preliminary threshold entrusting no task, but simply making someone a «clergyman»: makes him «enter the clergy». As Faivre writes again:

> «Existence of simple clerical state, without precise order, shows perfectly well that the cleric is no longer he who *carries out a* particular *function*, but he who is *part of a* privi-leged *establishment*»[52].

FAIVRE A., *Naissance d'une hiérarchie*, Paris Editions Beauchesne, 1977, 330-331: «*stipendium*», «*militare in castris dominicis*», «*aggreagari divinae militiae*»…
52 FAIVRE A., *Naissance d'une hiérarchie*, (Paris: Editions Beauchesne, 1977), 360. (Italics are mine).

In my modest opinion (and it is a structural judgment, independent of people's good and even excellent will), this way of conceiving and structuring is not healthy for the ecclesial ministry because it does not respond to the New Testament and because it deprives the ministry of its ecclesial character, since the ministers are no longer «men of the community», but in any case, *they are* the community, they are the Church, because they embody «the sacred» and for them are the rest[53]. In subsequent centuries, many people (including Ignatius of Loyola) would receive the «tonsure» not to perform any ecclesial service but to have certain privileges.

It would be wrong, then, to maintain this state of things, which must be overcome and which —as such a state of things— is independent of the holy or edifying life of real people. As an example of that time, the effort made by Saint Augustine in his time so that priests live in community with the bishop is, in itself, of great interest and probably did much good to many people; but seen in this context it probably contributed to strengthen this step from *function* to *status*.

A very eloquent aspect of this step is the evolution that took place, too, in relation to the monks in the desert. In the previous century, when monasticism appeared, the monks were not ordained, because they did not have a community in which to carry out a role. Hence they only participated in the Eucharist on special occasions. Then in the 5th century, the ordination of monks ordained «for themselves» became more frequent[54]. The famous Canon 6 of Chalcedon tried to stop this development, something which was aired again by the aforementioned work of Schillebeeckx[55]. But the truth is that Chalcedon was not able to stop such evolution, perhaps not just due to inertia but also because the so called «absolute» ordinations might have another legitimate significance[56]. In any case the passage from function to status is very clear.

---

53 A good proof is the social significance the word «Church» has acquired and the practical impossibility of understanding by this word something different from «hierarchy» (or sometimes the Pope alone). Everyone would recognize that, if that way of talking became *theoretically* legitimate, it would be heresy, as the Church is not just the hierarchy. But it is how language works in practice.

54 Cf. FAIVRE A., *Les laïcs aux origines de l'Église*, (Paris: Le Centurion, 1984), 226 and 232.

55 Cf. SCHILLEBEECKX E., *El ministerio eclesial. Responsables en la comunidad cristiana.* (Madrid: Cristiandad, 1983), 77.

56 Meaning that it is not about «ordination for themselves» but «entering a college» (of bishops or priests) and the responsibilities that go with that, since the ecclesiastical ministry derived from the Apostolate is intrinsically collegial. But one must recognize that this implies the real *assumption of ministerial tasks* in the community and in this sense, it is not «absolute» ordination anymore, but is referred to the ecclesial community it serves, even if this service is not performed in *a specific local community*. In relation to this, see RAHNER K., «The Bishop In The

Once the ministry is converted into status, the already useless «minor orders» will recover an unexpected (and distorted) function: they will become a sort of «no man's land», intermediate between hierarchy and laity. They are now not laity but clergy. But, as they are not yet committed to celibacy, these clergy contribute to the separation of the laity from «the sacred» and to the definitive sacralization of the «major» orders. If their functions lack objective it is not important, because the way through them is preparation for celibacy. They are not celibate, even though, if they marry, they are no longer «clergy» and go back to being lay.

In this way, celibacy, which previously had its basis in *service*, now moves toward a totally *cultic* foundation[57]. And it is explained thus: it is not demanded by the commitment to the community but by the «dignity of the altar». So ministerial celibacy will be associated with the advice given to married people about abstaining from sexual relations when they are to receive Holy Communion. And a real obsession will start to develop around the idea that lay people (who in some way are «impure» or, at least, profane) «should not touch what is sacred» (sacred chalices, etc.). In this way the zeal for sanctity we saw in the 4th century is now mechanized: it is not something for which the minister must labor but something he *already has* (or at least it is supposed he has) thanks to his celibate state, which sanctifies automatically. Left far behind are the reasons given by Pope Siricius, at the end of the last century, that they «are absorbed by the constant duties of their works[58]» among men.

As a quick conclusion: in the previous stage we saw an intensification of the aspects of «career», «sacralization» and (consequently) «separation». Instead the aspects of «experience» and «sanctity» have been reduced almost to the point of pure nomenclature. Of course, this could work in the difficult and obscure

---

Church» in *Theological Investigations*, VI, London: Darton Longman & Todd, 1974), 378f, 389f. That is: the rural missionary cannot have a parish assigned but he performs ministerial tasks; the bishop who is a bureaucrat in the curia does not perform episcopal tasks.

57 The reflection on the influence that this conception (linked with the vision of Augustine on sexuality and original sin) could have had, in fact, on the separation of women from almost all forms of ecclesial ministry will have to keep for later. But the connection between these factors intuitively appears very strong.

58 FAIVRE A., *Naissance d'une hiérarchie*, (Paris: Editions Beauchesne, 1977), 318. A comparison with death is valid: death is not worthy in itself, but love can lead up to it and make it very valuable. Celibacy in itself is not worthwhile either, but serving love can lead to it (as is shown much better by many feminine celibates).

situation of the 5th century, but it is clear that in the 20th century there is no way it can work.

4.2. **DECREASE IN POSITIVE BENEFITS**

Speaking about the 3rd century, we showed how the beginning of a greater structuring and rigidity of ecclesial ministry co-existed with a series of breathing spaces of liberty in the Christian community. Now we must say that this situation persists but is very reduced.

Anyway, the participation of the faithful in the election of the bishop is preserved. On this matter, Pope Saint Leo himself is a defender of ecclesial practice, even though material conditions make it more difficult sometimes. Not only because of the greater communication difficulties with the paralysis of civil life, but also because the appearance of the «Metropolitans» (of which we spoke when studying the 4th century) drove some to reserve for themselves the naming of «their» bishops. Saint Leo writes to one of them: «It is not legitimate for any Metropolitan to consecrate, on his own, someone as bishop, without the assent of the people and the clergy, instead he must put at the head of the Church he who has been elected by the whole city»[59]. And to Cyprian's arguments about the divine origin of this practice St. Leo offers some reasons of elemental governing common sense: «For as one who is well known and approved is sought out in peace, so must one who is unknown, when brought forward, be established by violence; (…) he who is to govern all, should be chosen by all», as the contrary will always be «material for dissension»[60].

That these phrases were not pure theory we can prove by the example of Innocent I at the beginning of the 5th century. This Pope thought that it was necessary to intervene in order to prevent some provinces electing as bishop a man of terrible notoriety who could even be a real criminal. Facing such an extreme situation the Pope intervenes. But his intervention is limited to a recommendation to the bishops and people of that province along the lines of choosing someone better and safer. He does not in any way impose a candidate, but leaves the election in the hands of those churches[61].

---

59 *Ep.* XIII,3 (PL 54,665). See also the next letter, n.6 (PL 54,673).
60 Cf. *Ep.* X,6 (PL 54,633-634). According to my knowledge the total intervention of the Pope in the naming of the bishops was not imposed fully until the time of Avignon. At that time the Popes were much in need of money to support the lavish court of Avignon and the bishop named by the Pope had to surrender a whole year of his rents…
61 Cf. FAIVRE A., *Naissance d'une hiérarchie*, (Paris: Editions Beauchesne, 1977), 326.

And something of this seems to remain legislated for in another work, important not in itself but because it very much influenced the Roman Pontificate and thus future legislation: the so-called *Statuta Ecclesiae Antiquae*, also from the 5th century.

The *Statuta* legally establish the distinction clergy/laity, as well as the degrees of the clergy (which with very few touches will pass in to the Good Friday liturgy and all the subsequent centuries). It also establishes definitively that there is no true «ordination» but from the diaconate onwards and that only the bishop has the power to ordain. We are, as we can see, in the ecclesial structuring that has survived until today. However, and in spite of the tendency toward hierarchy, the *Statuta* continue to mention laity when speaking about the appointment of bishops. So, Canon 11, which aims to obstruct a bishop from going from one See to another (in order to block eagerness to prosper and «careerism»), legislates that if in one case such a move were better for the good of the Church, «a decree should be presented to the Synod to be approved and signed by clergy and *laity*»[62].

And if in this issue of the election of bishops we still find these breathing spaces of liberty from the 3rd century, in other issues, however, we can perceive how some of these areas begin to shake. This is so for the legitimacy or illegitimacy of a lay person teaching in the presence of clergy. In the 5th century we find two opposing positions about this issue. The *Statuta* authorize it, following the early tradition, even though they establish the need for authorization by the clergy[63]. Instead Pope Saint Leo, in a letter to the bishop of Antioch, denies such a concession: preaching is the exclusive competence of «priestly ordination» and in the Church, as in the Body of Christ, it is advisable that each function be carried out by the proper person and that the inferior members do not perform tasks appropriate for superiors. It is interesting to note how the Pauline image of the «body» meant to be egalitarian in diversity has been ranked in this text, making it into a «ladder»[64].

---

62 See Cannon 11: «*Ut episcopus de loco ignobili ad nobilem per ambitionem non transeat, nec quisquam inferioris ordinis clericus. Sane, si id utilitas ecclesiae faciendum poposcerit, decreto pro eo clericorum et laicorum episcopis prorrecto, per sententiam synodi transferatur…*» (MUNIER C., (ed. Por), *Les Statuta Ecclesiae Antiquae*, París: PUF, 1960, 81).

63 Cf. Cannon 38: «*laicus, praesentibus clericis, nisi ipsis probantibus docere non audeat*». MUNIER C., (ed. Por), *Les Statuta Ecclesiae Antiquae* (Paris: PUF, 1960), 86.

64 «*Ut praeter eos qui sunt Domini sacerdotes, nullus sibi docendi et praedicandi ius audeat vindicare, sive ille monachus sive laicus sit, qui alicuius scientiae nomine glorietur. Quia, etsi optandum est ut omnes Ecclesiae filii quae recta et sana sunt sapient, non tamen permittendum est ut quisquiam*

The distinction between clergy and laity is complete. And for each concept a path can be identified which can be traced more or less in this way:

a) the concept of «clergy», from making reference to the universal priesthood of Christians, has moved on to refer exclusively to the triad bishop-priest-deacon, and later all the «tonsured»;

b) the concept of «laity», at the start, did not refer to anyone; then it described those in close proximity to the dedication of the clergy to the Church; later on it was used mainly to identify political power and, finally, it went on to designate all who were not of the clergy.

It remains only to put the detailed touches on this almost totally finalized clerical evolution.

5

The last touches of the clericalization of ministry

With the 6th century, in my opinion, the whole process we have described comes to a halt. This century will only add some touches. And the later evolution will only introduce some corrections demanded for the preservation (or unpredictable accidents) of that building we still inhabit.

We can divide our exposition into two sections. The first really is just a continuation of what we have seen in the last century, following history's inertia. About the second we could say that it leaves everything «officially» settled and concluded with the important reorganization of the Church and papacy undertaken, at the end of this century, by one of the greatest popes of the history of the Church: Gregory I.

5.1. FROM ECCLESIAL MINISTRIES TO HOLY FIGURES

Just as in the previous century, so in the 6th century vocations continued to diminish, in the end forcing Pope Gelasius (492-496) to accept the ever increasing reduction of the period of sojourn in each ministry, in order to make «recruitment» easier. To this we can add another new element, that is the birth (and de-

---

extra sacerdotalem ordinem constitutus, gradum sibi praedicatoris assumat, cum in ecclesia Dei omnia ordinata esse conveniunt ut in uno Christi corpore et excellentiora membra suum officium impleant, et inferiora superioribus non resultent» (Ep. 119: PL 54,1046 A; cf.also 1040).

velopment) of the papal bureaucracy, with the subsequent apperance of *administrative* functions (i.e. notaries, etc.), unknown until then.

The combination of both factors will intensify the primacy of the principle of «antiquity» over «aptitude», typical in all strictly hierarchical systems. Ironically, one could say that in the Church, too, the famous «Peter's principle» seems to have effect. As a consequence, the sociological image of the ministry has experienced change: from expressing a relationship between a specific function and the *ecclesial community*, it proceeds now to express the relationship of a function with a *particular individual*. The ecclesial ministry does not define primarily a certain task or a communitarian service (of teaching, assistance, or leadership, etc.) but expresses primarily the status of a person. Hence what our subtitle expresses: more than «performing roles», «holy figures are formed».

5.2.   FROM CLERGY TO ECCLESIASTICAL FUNCTIONARIES

This stage, as we just said, concludes at the end of the century with St. Gregory the Great (590-604) and his important reorganization of the papacy and the Church. But of this reorganization we could mention two aspects: one, more negative, which establishes the whole development we have followed; and another, more positive, which perhaps shows a certain consciousness of the negative elements of the said evolution.

a) Gregory I decides that all new administrative functions that crop up in the papal curia shall be embellished with all the titles of the dignity of those ministries or ancient orders which no longer had any liturgical or community function: the minor orders. So it comes about that to execute a merely administrative function in the papal curia *one must be a cleric*, one must be tonsured. As a consequence, these functions can no longer be accomplished by laity. In this way, imperceptibly, the «servants *of the Church*» become more servants of the *apparatus* of the institution rather than of the community. They will be the «ecclesiastics». This term covers more or less the same semantic field as «clerics» and designates those who have received tonsure.

b) But Pope Gregory's creativity goes further than the merely organizational. This Pope understands that the new situation in Europe supposes for the Church a *missionary* challenge: the Barbarians must be Christianized, not when they arrive in the cities of the ancient Empire, but in their native lands. Well-known are the actions of this Pope in sending missionaries (i.e. Saint Augustine to England), as well as the sensible and Christian instructions to carry out evangelization in a peaceful and inculturating manner instead of a violent and compelling one: do not pull down temples dedicated to other gods; do not destroy, but instead transform; do not invalidate social uses and customs of celebrations, anniversaries, etc. but instead make them «know inner joy»: because «with one stroke you cannot remove everything from fragile souls», nor «does one go up a mountain jumping but with slow steps»[65]. All this returns to the apostolic ministry its character of sending and ecclesial mission (as in Acts 13) and gives back to many ecclesiastics the apostolic meaning of their ministry, even though it does not always recuperate for that mission its official character of ministry due to the already bureaucratic and sclerotic situation of the «official» ministry.

But at least, as we have said, this important creative step helps to recover awareness of something which was tacitly valid in the new structuring of the ministries: that the ecclesial ministries, dominated by the need to «organize the Church» *had stopped being missionary.* Ever since the evolution started in the 3rd century, the bishops, all the time turning the Church and worship more inward-looking, had become less proclaimers of the Gospel and further from the image of the Apostles. And though this statement would not do justice to the 4th and 5th centuries, given the great theological quality of so many bishops and Fathers of the Church, who in this legitimate way exercised their apostolate and ministry, nonetheless, as A. Faivre underlines, even then it was an evident fact that *almost all* the conversions were achieved not by holders of ecclesial ministries but by those excluded from them: lay people (the entrepreneur who travelled, the slave sold and sent away, the military person made prisoner in a faraway land…)[66].

From then on something really curious has been happening in the Church: the men *more officially* entrusted with the task to «go out to the whole world and proclaim the Gospel to every creature» are precisely those who proclaim the Gospel less because a thousand other tasks and administrative worries prevent them. The community continues to be defined as «missionary», but those ultimately responsible for it are not so anymore, even, on occasions, they are not prepared for it because they know the «laws» of the Church much better than the human significance of the Gospel. They are also inhibited by an important lack of human contacts adequate for such an announcement, because their more

---

65 All these expressions come from this Pope's text to Augustine of Canterbury in the year 601. Cf. GREGORY I, «Cartas XI,56» (CC 140 A, 961. In PL 77,1215-1216, with different numeration).

66 Cf FAIVRE A., *Les laïcs aux origines de l'Église,* (Paris: Le Centurion, 1984), 212-227.

habitual circle of relations and their more immediate audience is made up of the supposedly more faithful «sheep», who almost look like the ones with less need of a pastor (sometimes even distant themselves from the society in which they live and from the hopes, joys, distresses and worries of the people of their times). Or, in any case, their relations with «the people outside» will be reduced to contacts with political powers with which one has «to negotiate» in certain situations or meet at «public» events...

Indeed, we find ourselves here very far from the image reflected by Jesus' life. This should be a cause for concern (and criteria for renewal) for all the ministers of the Church today. It would be very interesting if an agency specializing in statistics or sociological investigation could conduct a survey among all the bishops of the «First World» and ask them, for example, these two things: a) how many unbelievers, or at least non-Catholics, are in their closest circle of relations; and b) if there are some, is it a *personal* relation or does it derive simply from occasional encounters with political powers with whom they have had to relate or negotiate?

We do not say this ironically, but in any case with much distress[67]. What has been said is sufficient to show how the evolution we have tried to depict is practically closed and how it leads to a *strange clericalization of the ecclesial ministry which was born precisely trying to distance itself from all the clerical features*[68]. We can summarize this whole development with some precise words from Cardinal Yves Congar:

«Instead of being considered first of all as a service of (and in) the community to build up the Body of Christ, the priesthood is considered as a reality for itself, defined as a power personally possessed ("character") to consecrate the Eucharist. Absolute ordinations increased from the 9th century onwards and especially in the 11th century. Alexander III (Council of 1179, c.5) and Innocent III regulate them insisting that ordination entail a title of subsistence»[69].

67 Despite the criticism *of the way* in footnote 64 (Ch. 2), I have the impression that this same concern is revealed in the *fact*, and it is what is at the root, of the journeys of John Paul II.

68 Everything ecclesiastical oozes so much clericalism that it is sad to see how our Eucharistic prayers (resulting from the liturgical reform!) in the «prayer for the Church» entreat in detail for the Pope, one's own bishop (and the others') the presbyteral order ... and only dedicate a global mention (and not always) to the people, the real object of God's love and the main constituent of the Church, as if that faithful people were not deserving of too much inclusion alongside such «noble» figures... I know this is not the true interpretation of the fact, but it is undeniable that this interpretation is, without wishing to do so, the one that is most suggested.

69 CONGAR I., *Eclesiología desde san Agustín a nuestros días,* (Madrid: BAC, 1976), 103.

6

As an appendix

In the Early Middle Ages —with the loss of Latin and after the Carolingian Reform— the connection between ministry and worship, as we are already aware, ended with the loss of the perception of the Eucharist as the Supper of the Lord and an idea of the Mass as a marvelous spectacle more important to contemplate (from afar) than to participate in. Communion was rarely received: one assists only as «listener» («to hear» Mass).

But, in addition, throughout the Middle Ages there is a decline or corruption of the state of affairs described in this section when the ecclesial ministry assumes both political and economic powers. These latter («benefits», etc.) would tempt the Popes, who will end up trying to control all of them. In this way, one can say —even if it sounds anti-Christian— that «ministry» has turned into something like «benefit».

The details of that corruption are widely known. Let us just say, in this swift sketch, that this corruption normally has a double face: in the episcopate and in those who benefit, the corruption born of power or *corruption of the curia* (wealth, simony, economic immorality, distancing of the faithful…), and in the presbyterate (at least in the so called «lower clergy»), *corruption of negligence* (illiteracy, lack of most basic training, superstition, regular concubinage, etc.).

Also well-known are the innumerable voices which, throughout the Middle Ages, demanded the Church's reform. Not only heterodox voices or voices driven to heterodoxy because of the lack of understanding by the hierarchy (Waldensians, Hussites…), but also voices of saints and loyal and misunderstood faithful (Bernard, Catherine of Siena, etc.)[70]. Sometimes they tried to compensate this degeneration by the assimilation (or the escape) of the ministry into the religious life. But at other times the religious life itself was contaminated by the need of reform. An example of the former we have in the countless associations of clerics who, under the rule of Saint Augustine, swarm through Europe during the 11th century and are perhaps the most

---

[70] I have brought together impressive texts of these latter in *La libertad de palabra en la Iglesia y en la teología* (Santander: Sal Terrae, 1985; English version *Where the Spirit Breathes*, Maryknoll, NY: Orbis Books, 1989). As very eloquent details of where this ministry's «emphasis on cult» had arrived it will suffice to quote these two: priests called «altarists» who in the 15th century spent the day saying mass for a living, and the fact that —a short time before the famous thesis of Luther about indulgences— in Flanders it was possible to obtain these indulgences… as a lottery prize.

important endeavor in search of a life like the religious one, but not in «the peace of the countryside» but among the difficulties of the city.

Another more extreme example can be found in what happens to the phenomenon of the hermits who, in spite of their escape from the world, became «spiritual fathers» to many people, since the worldliness of the clergy made the «medical» (or mystagogical) function of the ministry impossible. We recall Robert of Arbrissel, Bernard of Thiron, Henri de Lausanne and many others, almost all of them ordained clerics, who —for evangelical reasons!— had abandoned the official exercise of their ministry and «scandalized» society with their miserable physical aspect («*pauper ego, mendicus ego*»). Many of these men were famed «soul directors», constantly visited. Curiously, eremitism incorporates at the same time both protest (sometimes incendiary) against the scandal of the clergy's riches, and the function of «spiritual (or mystagogical) direction», now aimed not just at the nobility, but also prostitutes, lepers and all other outcasts: one of the greatest claims of these hermits was that there was no need for «high birth» or a good education to achieve sanctity. And, curiously, in the same way that today we tend to present celibacy as a form of poverty (self-impoverishment, etc.), when sustaining it theologically, in that period so obsessed with «purity», poverty (or impoverishment) was presented as a form of purity.

In any case, this sketch is useful for noting one thing: something as characteristic of ministry as spiritual *help* is exercised now *outside* it and seen as not belonging to it. And without being so extreme, the refusal of Francis of Assisi to be ordained priest and the vow Ignatius of Loyola imposes on his own of not accepting bishoprics (in spite of the fact that Ignatius was a man more given to negotiation and the paths of possibility) are *in themselves* —and beyond the intentions of both characters— painful symbols of «something which definitively is not working» in ecclesial ministry.

But if we have quickly touched on this sad era, it was so we could add a word about the so-called «Catholic Reformation» and what it could mean for our subject. Trent carried out a reform of literally unthinkable seriousness and dimensions. But we must also recognize that it was done too late (as has happened so many times to the Church throughout its history). That is why it was a *controversial* reform. In addition to the reform, it was necessary to stand up to the Lutheran break-up and attacks. Controversy and self-defense gave the Tridentine Reform a certain partiality or one-sidedness: it was much more a reform of customs than of notions and structures. That is why it aimed more at recuperating the morality than the «Christianity» of the ministry as it is depicted by the New Testament. Because the New Testament had become by then the battlefield of the Protestants and the defense instinct typical of all controversy suggested it was dangerous to «play in the opponent's field»[71].

All this helps us to understand why the Tridentine Reform, as the only reforming theological option (and to combat what Luther wanted to regain from the New Testament), reinforced the «ontologization» and objectification of the ministry, which will no longer be immediately linked to the community but to the Eucharist (now also separated from the community and converted so many times into «private mass»); nor will it be defined by the Apostolate and the word, but instead by worship[72]. So «The seminaries helped to train the type of priest which is still familiar today; a man set apart from the world by his dress and way of life, who celebrates mass daily, says his breviary and is conscientious over his pastoral duties»[73].

Within this environmental frame I think it interesting to say a word about the classification proposed by J.M. Rambla about the three modes of understanding ministry in the post-Tridentine age. With this brief observation we conclude this appendix[74].

The three ways of understanding the ministry we will now expound all aim to be reforming. And Rambla believes they are embodied in these three tendencies:

a) One is more monastic; its motto, according to our author, could be: «sanctity and ministry». It continues the image of the ministry of Clicjtovec (to which Schillebeeckx attaches so much importance, as can be recalled[75]), and is embodied

---

71 The report Paul III entrusted to the Cardinals (Contarini, Sadolet, R. Pole…) already asked the Pope for a decentralization of so many powers as a condition for reforming the Church. But this did not happen, in the same way that a century before Martin V began to move away from the Council of Basle when it asked him to relinquish the right to reserve for himself the collations of the benefits. The stupid sterile concern for assembly procedure of that council facilitated things for him.

72 For this see the thesis of FREITAG J., (*El sacramento del orden en el concilio de Trento*) summarized by GRESHAKE G.,: «Freitag shows the tortuous paths followed by Trent about the theology of the ministry, paths that tend finally to place the bishop as the center of the ministerial issue. This means practically to *understand the ministry primarily as pastoral and directive ministry and not as a sacral-cultic service*. If after the texts approved by Trent they accented the sacral-cultic aspect it is because with the Roman veto the decree about jurisdictional issues had to be excluded and because of this only a minimal consensus was reached, precisely about the sacral-cultic competence of the ministry. The evolution after Trent that understands the ministry fundamentally from the sacral-cultic aspect represents a withering, understandable but not wanted by the council». GRESHAKE G., *Ser sacerdote*, (Salamanca: Sígueme, 1995), 219, (highlighting is mine). The author repeats the same explanation in a later much more extensive work: *Ser sacerdote hoy*, (Salamanca: Sígueme, 2006), 36. As one can see, the differences between the Roman Curia and the universal episcopate have not been issues only in the times of the II Vatican Council.

73 COMBY J., *How to Read Church History*, II, (London: SCM Press Ltd, 1989), 37.

74 What I say now has not been published due to the author's discretion. I have heard it from him in courses or seminar conversations.

75 Cf. SCHILLEBEECKX E., *El ministerio ecclesial. Responsables en la comunidad cristiana*, (Madrid: Cristiandad, 1983), 111-121.

preferably by those so-called «regular clerics» (Theatines, Barnabites, Somascans...) or priests who lived «*sub canone*».

b) Another, more ascetic, is represented by the French school (Bérulle, Olier, Saint John Eudes...) and its motto could be —according to our author— «sanctity *for* the ministry». This line of thought would be the one which would best incarnate the formula of «*alter Christus*» whose one-sidedness we showed in our first part. For this, the origin of the priesthood would be the need to give God worship fit for him, like the worship given him in the heavenly liturgy. And that is only possible for the human being through the Incarnation, which constitutes the Priesthood of Christ. (Which in itself is not incorrect: but now it is about an Incarnation that abstracts —and keeps apart from— human life and the historical destiny of the real Jesus).

c) Finally, another which is more missionary and which Rambla characterizes as «sanctity *in* the ministry», and in a ministry necessarily plural. Its motto would be «to help souls». And for that they will go on proposing ways of life which lead them into conflict with regular clerics and become concrete in aspects such as: mobility, plurality of tasks (which provides access to social activity and all those later discussions which continue today about it «belonging or not» to the ministry), non-local community, freedom in the face of many established practices (related, for example, to liturgy, customs, etc.). In general, the search for a ministry more relational than purely cultic. According to our author, in this last group we should locate Ignatius of Loyola and this would be one of the more important features of his historical significance: access to ministry, but breaking the mold that shaped it in his time. Whatever it can have been (something for historians to discuss), what is clear for us and for our study is that only this last form seems to maintain validity and meaningful opportunities for our world today. This is why I thought it useful to add this appendix.

Conclusions for today

« It seems to me that the comparison with the past shows that the present-day crisis of Christianity is unprecedented. Hence the need for the imagination in accessing power in the Church and to accept heroic remedies for what in concrete terms has to do with Roman power, that is, the invention of new ministries and the total rehabilitation of women».

J. Delumeau[1]

In these brief conclusions we would like, first of all, to carry out a sort of *evaluation* which would help us to clarify not the solution but *how to consider* today the subject of the ecclesial ministry. Secondly —and again taking up some criteria from the first part—, we would like to suggest a series of elements for a *spirituality* of ministry, which, in my opinion, will permit it to survive and to be lived to the full in a time of journey through the desert.

1

As a balance

1.1. THE CHURCH'S FREEDOM

A first thesis which seems to flow from our study is that, just as it has been transformed throughout history, so today, too, the shape of the ecclesial ministry can change and profoundly, too. Our study seems to suggest three reasons for this:

a) It can change, first of all, because both Scripture and Tradition leave the Church with a wide margin of freedom and wide room for maneuver. *The only binding thing for the Church, because it proceeds from Jesus, is the apostolate with a collegial structure and in communion with its head.*

b) It can change, secondly, because both history and the New Testament give a clear and constant example, sometimes of creativity, of knowing how to learn from historical realities and even of responsibility to history. The ecclesial tradition is never what Paul used to call a «work of the Law»: since the works of the Law neither save nor justify the human being (nor the Church), but instead destine it to despair. «All is permitted», even though what has to be seen is if «all builds up the Church», or paraphrasing Paul «what is it that builds it».

1 DELUMEAU J., «Une crise inédite» in *Le Monde*, Juin 5, 1979 (my emphases).

c) And it can change, finally, because not everything has been progress and growth in the evolution we have studied. The possible relapse into Old Testament models abolished by the fact of Christ, or the assumption of Neo-Platonic conceptions of hierarchy, or measures for emergencies to solve crises now overcome, are not things which should weigh down the Church, even though the Church could feel more comfortable with them «according to the flesh». But «the way of the Church is the human person»[2] and in no way is it the Sabbath. This means that we have to try to transcend the «Levitical» or «semi-Levitical» condition in which the ecclesial ministry finds itself at present, in order to try to configure it again «according to the order of Melchizedek».

These elemental considerations regain all their importance when we pay attention to the second element of this fourth section: the *today* in history and the responsibility the Church has in it. I would like to underline that we are not speaking of «today» in a sort of narcissism proper to these times, but in obedience to the signs of the times. This permits us to complete the previous idea with a second conclusion.

1.2. THE CHURCH'S RESPONSIBILITY

«Responsibility» is the obligation to respond. And the response of the Church is the Good News of Jesus for each age and the life which this Gospel can bring about in each new historical situation.

In response to this, I would dare to suggest as the thesis of this sub-section that *today the ecclesial ministry must set out on a process of change, and that it will not recover its identity by going backwards but by correctly marching forward.* As we said in the first part, the Church as revelation announces the reform of the Church-institution. There are at least three important reasons that can be used to prove this thesis.

a) The first is that in some documents of the Church we find already outlined a magnificent panorama for that change; for example, in the Third General Conference of Latin American Bishops, which took place in Puebla in 1979, where one can observe a clear concern for the mission and ministry of the Church. There it was said, as a starting point, something that is the starting point of all our reflection: «*the Church evangelizes, in the first place, through the global testimony of its life*». And as application of this principle, they added

---

2 JOHN PAUL II, *Redemptoris hominis 14.*

that each church and each community must be for the Latin American continent (and we can read: for our own country and for the whole world) an example of co-existence where

— liberty and solidarity pool together;

— authority be exercised in the manner of the Good Shepherd;

— a different attitude be lived toward wealth;

— organizational structures be tried out which allow more participation and open the way toward another more humane form of society;

— and «it be manifested that, without a radical communion with God in Jesus Christ, any other form of purely human communion is, eventually, incapable of sustaining itself and fatally ends turning against the human person» (#272 and 273).

Curiously, as we were commenting in the second part, this great program does not differ much from the one outlined by Paul in the *First Epistle to the Thessalonians*. The Pauline churches would recognize themselves in it, while we, Catholics, cannot be honest with people without acknowledging that this great program seems to have been left in the loft of good intentions and that actually the Church, too frequently, does not evangelize with the global testimony of its life. And this not only because of the unavoidable harshness of reality and the classical and Virgilian «*lacrimae rerum*», but because we are too much the prisoners of a notion which canonizes all that has happened without discerning it before the Lord. In my opinion, the text of Puebla regains life and light when it is read within the perspective of all the development presented in this work.

b) The second reason that seems to compel a profound change is the necessary effort to read the signs of the times; a reason presented in the brief words, at the beginning of this chapter by the French historian, which speak of things like «heroic remedies» or «imagination in accessing power in the Church».

For any present day historian, the significance in the 16th century of the invention of the printing-press or the compass, the discovery of America and the re-discover of the Greek-Latin culture, are easy topics on which to comment. They were all tremendously important historical changes which gave rise to a whole new world. But when entering that world the Church was first sick and later on divided into two churches, both maimed, both lame, both one-eyed...

Well, today, too, other signs of the times exist. The sociological de-Christianization of the «First World» (inevitable at this moment, even if we could still continue to discuss about who is really responsible), with the ensuing transformation of its churches into minority diaspora communities; the end of the ecclesiastic «Euro-centrism» which implies the return of the churches of the East to dialogue with the great Asian religions; the «bursting in of the poor» into the churches of Latin America, etc., all these are factors of a different world which are more novel and radical than the ones mentioned taking place in the Renaissance. And they are factors which have grown and broadened in the brief time elapsed between the first and second edition of this book.

If we really accept that the mission of the Church is more important than the Church itself, I do not think it too presumptuous to state that the ecclesial ministry can and should let itself be led meekly by the Spirit of God to a profound reform or to an Abrahamic exit «of homeland and kin» toward the new land where the Lord will lead it and where its own lost identity lies. And I make this statement knowing that any time a scholar starts to perceive the ideals formulated put into effect, he immediately distances himself from these aims and ends up saying the famous: «No, not that…not that!». That harsh destiny forms part of the Abrahamic path or of the path of the people of Moses, a road slower than the one of individual consciences, but one that does not annul the command of the God of history.

In face of the enormity of the historical imperatives of evangelization in our days, it will not be an exaggeration to suspect that the ecclesial ministry, due to the immense wear and tear resulting from rubbing against history, has perhaps ended up structurally focusing more on its own care than on following Jesus. And, in addition, it has used its gradual sacralization to affirm that caring for itself was no longer following Jesus. From this has emerged a Church which, as in the «Pastoral Epistles», lives always more aware of its inward settlement than of its outward mission. This point is, I think, decisive for understanding the imperative to recover the ecclesial ministry's evangelical identity. This is what we have tried to do in these pages: to really have Jesus Christ as the center of the Church and not the hierarchy, as necessary as the latter may be. For this reason I will digress once more to show the consequences for the *present day* Church of the evolution which for centuries has taken place in the ministry.

Since Christianity was wiped out and the Church stopped being what shaped society, the development of the ministry we have tried to describe has been transforming the Church much more into a *decorative* rather than *questioning element* in society.

This is the challenge today for the Church. And I call it «challenge» because this situation is, *at the same time,* serious and comfortable. To be a decorative element will always produce acceptance for the Church, but it will not mean that the Church be taken into account. The ecclesial ministry will be used as the flowers at weddings, baptisms or burials… and other intense or wretched moments in life. But when this ecclesial ministry speaks of the «option for the poor» or of the God of justice, or of serious and urgent reforms of the social and economic order… then so little attention will be paid to it (or even less) as when it speaks of «not using the pill», to use a very current example, and without entering into the discussion about the degree of correctness of each of these teachings.

And attention paid will be even less if the ecclesial ministry affirms all this merely as a *noble exhortation* to the powers that be and not as a call to those oppressed to regain their dignity and the management of their own destinies. We must acknowledge that the ecclesial ministry tends to speak in the former manner because the latter would sound like confrontation and be frightening not only for society but even for the Church.

So if the ecclesial ministry wishes to be in society not a decorative element but a factor of confrontation it will only find rejection, because people battle a lot against being confronted by God's radicalism. Rejection will come in the first place from the very representatives of the ministry who will resist that confrontation, too. Also, on the part of the most powerful sector of society which continues to believe a saying attributed to Mussolini about the ecclesial ministry (whether they believe or not): «I take care of the people from birth until death and then I hand them over to the Pope». If the ecclesial ministry were to accept that role it would find a certain acceptance and social peace and would feel tempted to think that peace to be a *better* situation for carrying out the ecclesial role and that in the long run it could be put to good use, etc., etc. But it would not perceive that what is being offered is in reality to be recognized on condition that it renounces Jesus' Good News and be content with proclaiming it to itself.

That is why the necessary reform of the ecclesial ministry will be slow, consequent and hard-fought, as was the path of the primitive Church. Here, persecution has to be expected, even if it is not sought. It will be necessary to proceed «with fear and trembling» (and not with comfortable joy) in order not to make mistakes which can damage the cause being served. This cause is today a command of the Lord. For if the Church accepted in future society to be just a decorative element and not a questioning (or «fermenting») element its mission would be ended. And to it could be applied the famous phrase of Nietzsche:

«What are the churches for if not as tombs and monuments to God?».

But the Church is not called on to be tomb but sacrament; and not of any god, but the God Father of our Lord Jesus Christ.

c) The third reason is an «ecumenical» reason. The present separation of the churches is one of their greatest sins. In the re-union of the churches rests almost the only serious possibility for Christians to continue carrying out today their evangelizing mission. On the other hand, there have already been important ecumenical documents «of agreement», one in 1973 and another in 1986; they should not remain as mere scraps of paper[3]. These documents have not been studied here for lack of space, but at least they have been present as an ultimate horizon in this work. The reform of the ministry is, also, an ecumenical imperative because one can say that in the structure of the ecclesial ministries resides today almost the only serious *objective* obstacle obstructing the re-union of the churches[4].

1.3. THE CHURCH'S GOAL

But it is possible that, even accepting the thesis above, the path to take will still remain obscure and divisions among Christians arise again. In a way it should be like this: because the ways of God have never been clearly traced beforehand; both Abraham and Moses and his people, or the Apostles after Easter, or the great saints of the Church, almost always started out «not knowing where they were going» (Heb 11:8). This does not imply, however, that one cannot in some way glimpse the direction of the road. And keeping in mind all the evolution

---

3 Of the agreements in the so-called «Dombes Group» we cite the one in 1973 (*Pour une réconciliation des ministères*), the one in 1976 (*Le ministère épiscopal*) and the one in 1986 (*Le ministère de comunión dans l'Église universelle*).

4 Paul VI had the daring honesty to admit in public, in 1967, that precisely that ministry whose reason for being is the unity of the Church was the major obstacle for the union of Christians. This paradox describes, in my opinion, the present situation of all ecclesial ministries: a way of conceiving their identity which makes their mission almost impossible. Notwithstanding the fact that «all be one» is without doubt more the will of God than a maximalist reading (and not the only one) of Matthew 16.

studied, I think we could entitle the glimpsed goal of that road by inverting a phrase from the author of the aformentioned *Traditio Apostolica*: Hippolytus wrote in the 3rd century that the time had come to pass «from charity to tradition». Now is the time for the Church to pass from tradition to charity. I will try to explain in more detail what I believe this means.

1.3.1. *TO MAINTAIN THE EVOLUTION SET OUT IN STRUCTURING*
To start with, going from tradition to charity does not mean in any way that we favor a total break with Tradition, which would mean an illusory start from zero and signing up for all sorts of spontaneous claims, making into proofs what are only suggestions and demonstrations what are only calls for more profound studies. We have already acknowledged those dangers into which we fall sometimes nowadays.

That is why we repeat that the fact that the Church needs a structure is for us evident and calls for obedience. If it did not need that structure it would not need people responsible for it either and we would not here be reflecting on the ecclesial ministry. But then the Church would end up being easy victim to all manipulators of whatever sign who only serve themselves, like one of those prophets in the *Didaché* which we saw in the third part and who today could use the mass media for their business. So, the evolution we have studied should be respected inasmuch as it is a process for structuring the ministry.

Respected yes, but that does not mean that it cannot be corrected.

1.3.2. *PEOPLE WITH SERVICES INSTEAD OF SACRED POWER*
And how it should be corrected is suggested by a three-fold step which appears in the tradition we have studied which now we must examine more slowly:

a) To go from *charism to posts or positions* is something understandable and almost necessary in a growing Church that wishes to be «catholic».

b) To go from *post to career* is much more ambiguous and something that should be avoided, even if inertia in this point may be very difficult to overcome.

c) But to go from *career to sacred status* (or self-sacralization) is something to be avoided at all costs, even at the structural levels and independently of the possibility that later people manage to resist that structural temptation. If there is something Christological in the ecclesial ministry, as we will immediately see, it is this obligation to follow the same trajectory as Christ Jesus shedding his divine image, assuming the image of the servant, presenting himself as a man like any other and obeying God until the death of his own «sacred ego» (cf. Phil 2:6ff). Because of this, any endeavor to overcome the «crisis of vocations» by returning to the ministry its clerical brilliance will end converting the churches into «tombs of God» as Nietzsche said. The true direction points toward having the ministry correct that historical distortion it went through: *from being mission of service to being personal dignity...* This would be a first criterion for correction.

From here and in keeping with the trajectory of Jesus we just mentioned, the ministry will also correct the other historical distortion it went through: *from being ecclesial to being clerical.* This will be our second criterion for correction. Recovering the identity of the ministry will entail getting rid of that unjust private appropriation by us «priests» of the notion of «church», in order to regain the theological notion of «People of God» and also of the ecclesial ministries as services within that people. That is: to put in effect the famous revolution Vatican II conducted —theoretically— when it inverted the order of chapters 2 and 3 of *Lumen Gentium,* to speak initially to the people and then to the ministries that serve them, instead of speaking first to the «sacred power» and then to the people as a terrain for the exercise of that power.

It is said that J.A. Möhler summarized in this way the ecclesiology that he had been taught: «God has founded the hierarchy and thus has given us all that is necessary until the end of time»[5]. Well, what we are trying to say is that all the necessary renewal of the ecclesial ministry depends on leaving behind such ecclesiology. The Church is not the «Mystery of the sacred power» (for which afterwards one will have to look for some «lay people» who can be the subject of such sacred power); it would not even suffice to say that the Church is «a sum of lay people plus sacred power». The Church is simply the unfathomable mystery of the *People of God* (reflection of God one and triune), *missionary in History,* and, because it is in history, that people needs some persons responsible to teach them, to feed them and to direct them in their life and in their mission. This principle must be the guiding light of all renewal. But since all of us have some ministry in the Church, this principle is more uncomfortable than the other hierarchical ecclesiology. This explains our frequent resistance to turn to it.

5 Cited by COMBLIN F., *El Espíritu Santo y la liberación.* (Madrid: Paulinas, 1987), 205; also ESTRADA J.A., *Del misterio de la Iglesia al pueblo de Dios,* (Salamanca: Sígueme, 1987), 220. The phrase which comes from the recension of a history of the Ancient Church published in 1823 in the journal of Tübingen, was rescued, if I am not mistaken, by KUNG H., in *Estructuras de la Iglesia.* (Barcelona: Estela, 1965), 310.

Finally, a third criterion of correction and renewal consists in the ministry trying to return *from the vertical structure* it has acquired throughout its history to the *collegial structure* it received from Jesus. With this we take up another of the commitments of Vatican II: together with Church-People of God, collegiality. But a collegiality which —as was also said during Vatican II— must take place not only between the Pope and the bishops, but *at all levels* of the exercise of ecclesial ministry; this is what they tried to maintain in the 3rd century when the ministries began to be structured (as we said in III, 2.3.2).

The college undoubtedly has a head and this is not questioned at all. But what is needed is that the head be head only and that it does not pretend to be body, too. The Pope cannot say: «I am the episcopal college» nor can he act as if he thought this was so. Neither can the Bishop say: «I am the presbyterate», or the parish priest think: «I am the parish council». And it is well known that we human beings tend to act like this... But Saint Bernard reminded Pope Eugene III —who had been his pupil— that this was equivalent to converting the body of Christ into «a head with fingers».

I do not deny that working with a collegial structure can entail thousands of practical difficulties (not just because of competencies, but also because of the necessary speed some decisions can frequently demand). Right now we will speak of the problems which have been actively impacting on the evolution of the ministry and will re-appear time and again. But in doing so we must also add that a collegial structure is one of the most necessary things for the Church to «evangelize with the global testimony of its life», and it is a form of self-deceit to pretend that this collegiality exists when «unconditional support» for decisions taken alone are sought *a posteriori* (and with pressure)...

In summary then: in the return *from clerical to ecclesial, from personal dignity to service and from vertical to collegial* we have three criteria very much in the line of the New Testament and it is very important to correct what needs correction in the historical evolution of the ministry so that it can move «from tradition to charity». If we applied these criteria, precisely what Jesus said about the Temple in Jerusalem could happen: that a priesthood «work of human hands» would be replaced by another priesthood which would not be the work of such hands. This is because power and self-sacralization are, evidently, the work of human hands and service and self-giving are the work of God alone.

Once this has been established, one should know that when it is time to be oriented toward that «beacon», the Church will be confronted with a series of problems never totally resolved and about which one could show how they also remained latent conditioning the evolution we have described and how they will be there conditioning our future quests. Without pretending to be exhaustive I will mention only some of them. And trying not to lengthen the list of problems, I will limit myself to offering some orientation about them in fine print.

a) The question about the *character of Christianity: for masses or for minorities?* A question already dormant in the passage of time from the 2nd to the 4th century or from the situation of the Barbarians to be converted to «Christianity».

In my view, Christianity will always be a minority in fact, but it cannot renounce being for everyone, converting that fact into a right. When this happens, all those distinctions between «laity» and «states of perfection» are born. And we should ask ourselves if they are not a hidden form of Gnosticism which has again introduced into the Church its distinction between «pneumatic» and «psychic» human beings. The minority character of Christianity is more along the line of the «vicariousness» or of the communion of saints (the intrinsic communitarian character of all that is Holy). But this minority does not coincide at all with that of the ministers in relation to the people! To that minority belong many «poor and humble people» to whom God communicates the secrets of his Kingdom still hidden from many learned and governing people.

b) The problem of the *dialectic between local church and universal Church* which we already found in the dual ecclesiology of *1 Corinthians* and *Ephesians*.

The goal of this dialectic is to configure the Church as «community of communities». And I think that if, in the early centuries that discussion logically came down on the side of the local churches until the awareness of «catholicity» began to take hold, today, owing to the inevitable course of history, such discussion tends to overlook the importance of the church at local levels and a recovery of the New Testament theology of the local churches is much needed. It cannot be that in the «catholic» Church any local church gives the impression of being the «backyard» of the Vatican. And we do give that impression. In this dialectic, the ecclesial ministry has much to do as the simultaneous *bond* between the diverse communities and within each community. Here we find in germ the *collegial* character and the *local* character of the ecclesial ministry.

c) The *character for service inherent* in every ecclesial community: the Church is only Church when it exists «for the human being»; «a Church that does not serve, serves as nothing» and so ecclesial communion is not only *koinonía* of life inwards but even more *koinonía* of mission outwards.

It could be convenient to quote again two phrases of Pius xi and of K. Barth which express the insight of this character of the Church precisely in our 20th century: «Human beings have not been created for the Church, rather the Church has been created for human beings» (Pius xi, *Speech to Lenten Preachers*, February 1927). In the Encyclical *Rerum Ecclesiae*, Pius xi repeats again: «The Church does not exist for the number of its members but above all for human beings». And now the phrase of K. Barth: «If the Church has no other object than that of its own service then it carries in itself the stigma of death»[6]. Or as Bishop Gaillot entitled a book: *A Church that does not serve, does not serve at all.*

d) The *tension between* the unavoidable *historical servitude* of the Church and its obligation to be *eschatological happening,* whether we give this the name of «sacrament of salvation», «alternative community» or «leavening community». This is another factor which has been present from the beginning of our evolution, with an undeniable tendency to fall more on the first side of this dialectic than on the second.

Perhaps the Church is the institution in which measures taken in emergencies tend to remain unaltered for centuries. I would like to comment on this point using a personal confession, given that practically all the readers of this work will be brothers in the faith and in the Church: speaking with unbelievers, I have sometimes heard that for them it would be truer to say that some democratic societies are «alternative communities» in relation to the Church and not the other way round. At least, because (in spite of the tremendous thickness of everything human) they still search for their own

---

6 BARTH K., *Esquisse d'une dogmatique,* (Genève: Labor et Findes, 1984), 184. All this has to do with the intrinsically missionary character of the Church that today is dangerously devaluated and insufficiently made clear, because we tend to think that the mission consists more in «defeating» and gaining the other one for us, than in helping this person to do good. We confuse mission with mere proselytism.
In any case, I think we have to say that, in the faith community, all responsibilities —and demands— «*ad intra*» could be, in fact, more visible and meaningful, but adding that, by rights, they are secondary.

improvement as societies, while the Church seems to them anchored in the models of the «*Ancien Régime*», which it has «canonized» as the will of God for it. It is undoubtedly a harsh accusation and it comes «from outside»; but it should challenge us as believers.

e) The need to re-examine more slowly the current validity of the *connection between presidency of the Eucharist and presidency of the community*, a connection which has been in place since the 3rd century (but not before). The advantages and coherence of this I already underlined. Now, that coherence remains only when it is not forgotten that, for the Christian, the *thysia* pleasing to God is «to build community» (let us again remember Heb 13:10) and that this is what has been made possible through the Eucharistic offering.

Related to this is the question if the Christian Eucharist, in its «visible» elements has not lost too much *Christian* specificity so as to be assimilated too much to the generic-religious category of «worship». But it should be equally clear that when I speak of «re-examining the validity of that connection» I am not implying in any way that the Eucharist does not need some minimal requisites in order to really be Eucharist «*of the Church*». This was already established in our historical analysis. And in this sense I find foolish the activities of some groups closed in on themselves who supposedly form «Christian communities» and thereby feel «self-sufficient». It is true that any community has the right to the sacraments and that this is a primary right not sufficiently honored today; but it is also true that it does not have that right «in any way whatsoever» and that not any group of baptized friends is now a community *of faith*. A different avenue is that perhaps we, before excommunicating these attempts without redress, should wonder why they take place and what portion of blame our comfortable immobility has in that uneasy radicalism.

f) And finally, the enormous *factual plurality of the culture and the Church today*, which again makes more urgent the early concept of ministry as a factor of unity and raises the question of how to exercise the ministry in *this real Church* without confusing the unity of the Church with the proper one-sidedness of every human being nor trying to eliminate plurality by easy excommunication (useless in the end).

This great factual plurality is not just a negative fact, even though at times it can seem excessive and even unhealthy. It is the fruit of a recovery of what is *essential* in the Christian faith, which relativized many remnants from baroque times (this being produced as an effect of Vatican II). It is also fruit of a greater presence of «eschatological caution» in the consciousness of the Church, which is shown, for example, in the statement that «no party exhausts the totality of what is Christian». This statement has been the basis of the pluralism of political options for the faithful. Another thing is that this pluralism should try to be guided by undoubtedly Christian criteria, such as the preferential option for the poor or the search for the maximum respect for the dignity of all people. But the fact is that such pluralism exists today *de facto* and not only in the field of political options. And that it is a terrible way of exercising the ecclesial ministry to try to eliminate such pluralism by decree, as some are trying now.

The existence of all these almost eternal problems does not mean that today there are not sufficiently concrete opportunities for action and tasks or first steps to take in the new configuration of the ecclesial ministry. As an example (and of course from my individual thoughts and personal feelings) I would also like to indicate some of these.

1.4. ROADS TO OPEN

In my opinion, the Church today could bring *real* ministry nearer to what is *official* ministry. It should also try to approach more that communion in plurality which characterized the Pauline churches[7]. And it should look for more missionary, less turned inward forms of ministry in the Church. The examples I will now suggest, somewhat tentatively, try to cover that triple route.

To begin with, it cannot be denied that today in the Church there are many real «ministries» without ordination or any type of «installation». And also many are ordained not to exercise any ministry at all: sometimes to lock themselves up in some task which can be very noble (like, for example, that of scientific researcher), but which in itself is not an *ecclesial* ministry. At other times perhaps only to be at a «level of dignity» which will permit them to speak «officially» to someone else on that same level… Here is very much reflected that step of going from «function to status» which has appeared throughout our historical vision

---

7 Plurality —we have already said— is a sign of our times, and in it the Church will only be a reflection of our world. But communion (in that plurality) is the great need of our world and in it the Church could become a little more sacrament of salvation.

and which left many of those functions without anyone to perform them or in the hands of people to whom they were not officially assigned.

As a consequence of this, the ministry which —in its last form of presbyterate and episcopate— ended absorbing all the other functions, could today, at least in some cases, detach itself from some of these, not to restore ministries that now have no validity, but to give way to the appearance of new ministries.

A small example (though very visible) of that absorption is what happened with the readings in the Eucharistic celebration. The time came when even the readings were done by the «priest», the only actor in that celebration and who was no longer called «presider» but «celebrant». Suddenly, after the timid reform of Vatican II, some «non-official» lectors have started to appear. This example has only symbolic value, as reading is something practically anybody can do today[8], and for this reason it does not need to be acknowledged as an ecclesial function. But, maybe, something similar should occur with other ministries which I think are really ministries even if they are not recognized as such. I will give a pair of examples.

a) After the failure of the timid attempt to restore the diaconate by Vatican II, it would be interesting to consider if this restoration could not consist in acknowledging those brothers and sisters who are exercising in the Church a real *diakonía*. The description in *Acts* (6:1ff) shows that the problems of «material help» were assigned to the diaconate. In this sense, the real *diakonía* of faith today is the fight for justice, so, should not a recognised «diaconate» exist nowadays for those to whom the Church has given tasks of this kind? Bodies like «Justicia y Paz», «Tutela Legal», «Human Rights», movements focusing on Young Christian Workers (JOC)… embody today an important *diakonía* of the churches conducted usually by lay people, women and men. Are they not the *real* deacons of the churches now? And so, should not their ministry be officially established? This, of course, would not signify their clericalization, as it is about new forms of ecclesial ministry which will go beyond the duality clerics/laity to be substituted by community/ministries.

b) Another example: in many churches of Latin America, in places where there is almost no clergy, there are a good number of religious women and «delegates of the Word» or other pastoral workers who perform true ecclesial functions, even if they do not consecrate the species (in some regions of Spain we are finding similar situations).

8 At least in comparison with the 3rd century; but many times now the worry about what others may think or paying more attention to oneself than to those listening can bring about unintelligible readings.

Their role is sometimes truly important for the Church and even more effective than an almost totally absent humdrum clergy. Why do we not make as a structural part of the Church what already exists and works? And when I speak of establishing them as official ministries I am not advocating the mere institution of a new rite which would only add a few pages to the Roman Ritual, I support that this new rite be an expression of a new ecclesial attitude and self-understanding. These new ministries should not be absorbed or substituted again by the «presider of the Eucharist» the moment this person appears, just because «the priest knows everything and understands everything»...

c) Finally, hoping for a full recovery of all aspects of the ecclesial ministry, we would have to add that one of its most deficient tasks today is that function that used to be called «spiritual direction». In Bloch's terminology, so many times mentioned, a function in between doctors and poets. Clearly it is not a task that could be assigned by decree, but a charism prudently recognized. However, I must confess that one of the most negative symptoms of the Church today is, in my opinion, the lack of true «teachers of the spirit», of authentic mystagogues, of that discrete companion (more than a commanding director) who knows how to promote the authentic experience of the Spirit, how to nurture it, how to accompany and make it grow, bear fruit, while the director discreetly fades away. Our «curates» (pay attention to the meaning of the word) normally know everything except caring and *curing*: at most, we have correct answers of moral casuistic or canonical possibilities, or ready-made recipes of «*counseling*» or of group dynamics, etc., etc. But who really knows how to teach to pray and to love? That is: we can be *experts* on techniques, but this does not yet mean that we are *teachers of the spirit*. It is clear that this is one of those charisms where the saying that «*Salmantica non praestat...*» applies. But, in spite of everything, we should ask ourselves if such a lack is not a disturbing symptom of the absence of the experience of the Spirit in ourselves (and one can surmise that the training received in seminaries must have some responsibility in this ...). The surprising attraction and success of all sorts of «gurus» and oriental teachers is a clear demonstration that people need teachers of the spirit and since they do not find them in the Church, they look for them elsewhere.

These examples are only the first steps to start walking. Problems will arise (like the temporal character of many ecclesiastical ministries, which would also express their character as «functions» more than of «states»). But the road must not be drawn *a priori*, but by discerning (and when convenient recognizing it as such) what the Spirit seems to be brewing in the Church as valid answers to historical needs.

To make clear some of the things said, I would like to remember how Saint John Baptist De La Salle explained to his disciples that education is a *ministry* comparable to that of the Apostles, the bishops or the doctors of the Church, and precisely for that reason it required total dedication; that was the reason why he did not permit his followers to receive ordination as priests, because in that case one of the ministries would suffer. Perhaps today there would not be such time incompatibility (in fact many «curates» perform perfectly well their ministry and know how to combine it with another sort of personal profession or dedicated task). But, in spite of everything, the Saint had reason in both the ecclesial vision which «diversified» ministries and in the ministerial vision which assigned such character to education[9].

d) I would like to present a final example which is surely controversial, but for me has a lot to do with the possibility of a more missionary and less «conservative» disposition of the episcopal ministry. I refer to the appointment of bishops. Our century has practically seen the end of a historical stage in which Rome finally —slowly, century by century— could *rescue* the faculty of appointing the bishops from worldly powers (kings, chiefs of State and other forms of «patronage») and recover this right for the Church. This is something to be thankful for. But history does not end there. Once that recovery has been made, I think the moment has come to *give back* those appointments (at least in some important degree) to the local churches and what happens many times is that —through prerogatives and concordats— Rome returns part of that recovered right to civil powers. Well, Jesus said that the only true shepherd is the one who enters through the door of the sheepfold, while the one who climbs up another way is a thief and a robber (Jn 10:1). And today there are too many appointments in which the shepherd enters «climbing up another way». The earlier practice, in which there was more intervention by the people and the neighboring bishops, constitutes for the Church not only a curious historical memory, but a moral imperative. And a grave moral imperative, not only through faithfulness to the apostolic tradition evoked by Saint Cyprian, but rather for the reasons of common sense presented by Saint Leo. The current procedure is theologically possible and legally correct, but that does not mean that it is theologically the *only* possible one, nor the more perfect morally speaking. That is why I dare to repeat (with no authority of course except

9   This is so when education is understood as *development of the human being* in the liberation of liberty and not as a mere collection of technical teachings. In the first sense it is something that has to a lot with faith and that was what gave Jesus the title of «Master».

that of truth and love, aware that one cannot wish anything better for the Church than that it get closer to Jesus) that the Popes have here a moral imperative, and a serious one at that. I do not advocate for a total disappearance of Rome's role, but for a greater participation of local churches. Rome would have a word to say, its role of arbiter when needed… But all these legal particulars are outside the frame of this work.

The aim of the above was to provide a series of possible examples of something which today is perceived as the call of the Spirit and which —precisely because of that!— does not appear as a totally formulated path or as a recipe or a «*prêt-à-porter*» solution. It could also happen that everything that has been said will only seem like the stupid advice of a pretentious person. But what moves this pretentious one is *the possibility that the Good News be proclaimed to the people today*, which is something the structure itself of the ecclesial ministry seems sometimes to prevent.

It is a well-known fact that the great cultural changes modify also the theophanic mediations or analogies through which human beings can glimpse or surmise what is called «God». And today we find ourselves before one of those great cultural changes which could be imagined so: power no longer seems theophanic but anti-divine. The platonic scale of hierarchies which caused such admiration in the Areopagite does not reveal God today, while fraternity, equality and respect act as very real mediations. These could suggest to the human person today that everything which Jesus announced of God is true.

Such change is permitted and *encouraged* by the Gospel itself. The only thing needed is that we ecclesiastical people have «ears to hear». But when we human beings get anchored in other eras and in other mediations we do not perceive that and, even with goodwill, see only blasphemies where God «leaves his mark».

Meanwhile, only a profound spiritual experience of the ecclesial ministry will enable us to continue our voyage through crisis waters without floundering in the first storm or being left hibernating in the past. This is the last point to conclude.

A spirituality of surrender[10]

In this last part of our conclusion we do not ask any more about the concrete functions which make up the ministry. We have seen many times in these pages —particularly in the conclusions of the second section— that such functions could be grouped around the *word* (that is, evangelization, teaching or preaching, which perhaps correspond to the early «apostles», «doctors» and «prophets»), around *assistance* (with its double stream: material and spiritual, typified in the «physicians» and «poets» of Bloch and which today should surely increase), around *direction* (presider of the Eucharist and presider of the community). All this is part of the missionary task of the Church.

We do not wonder now either about the *way for «distributing» and structuring* these functions. We have already insisted, too, that on this issue there would be many things to reform and new structures to explore in the present Church.

What we are wondering about now is *the way to live* those ecclesial functions. This is what constitutes its «spirituality». And it is possible *now today*, even with structures which are far from ideal and in crisis. Moreover: it is not only possible, but it is a condition for any reform and any recovery of the ministry's identity.

I would like to reflect on the notion of *spirituality of surrender*. The real worship and sacrifice of Christ consists in this says the *Letter to the Hebrews*: on the donation of one's own life to the life and mission of the community. This is the moment to take up again something we said in the first section when speaking of the new priesthood of Christ. If we wish to equate the ecclesial ministry with a «priestly» function this *cannot be done from the general religious category of «priesthood»* (which ended with Jesus and cannot be reborn without making Jesus void), *but from the vital and existential route of the Messiah,* the one which converted him into «priest of a new order»: his life given up unto death, by which he reconciled the world with God, or «in the heavens a minister in the sanctuary and in the true tabernacle, which the Lord pitched, not man» (Heb 8:1-2).

---

10 For a theological basis of this spirituality, I refer to «the biblical notion of election» in GONZÁLEZ FAUS J.I., *Proyecto de hermano. Visión creyente del hombre,* (Santander: Sal Terrae, 2000³), 671ff.

According to the *Letter to the Hebrews*, this life of Jesus has two characteristics which constitute the two attributes of his priesthood: we have a *merciful and trustworthy* priest (cf. Heb 3:1ff and 4:14ff)[11]. The life of Jesus as life-for-others or as Mercy of God put into action («pro-existence», the expression made popular by H. Schurmann). And precisely because of this, «trustworthy» in a double sense: a) that the God of Jesus is the only credible one for humanity (facing all other innumerable gods of reason or desire, defined as «Being», «Motor», «Power»…, but not as «Love») and, also, b) that in the man-Jesus all human persons are credible before God.

This type of life, according to the *Letter to the Hebrews*, is impossible for human beings: as «law of life» it is only made possible «through the eternal Spirit of God» (9:14). But, after Jesus and with him, the servant can place in the Church small signs of that life. And, according to this, the ecclesial ministry should become the great respecter of humanity[12], emptying itself of its «ecclesiastical» image, just as Christ shed his divine image, and putting love for the community totally above love for its own caste.

In this way, the ecclesial ministry should feel challenged to be ahead of any other institution in all that can signify defense of the dignity of the human person and in support of what today is called «human rights» —particularly the rights of the poor who are the most sacred. These institutions only endeavor to make concrete that divine dignity of the children of God. I refer to what was said about the conclusions of the New Testament (2,7). We do not need to add that even today we are far from this goal, and that many «human ministries» (that is: non-ecclesial) are ahead of us in this.

Accordingly, one of the things which needs more spirituality in the ecclesial ministry is the constant effort so that the «service of the altar» or the service to the necessary «bureaucracy» do not substitute in any way the service to *the community of persons*. To be ordained, all candidates must know (as we said in 2,7.2.1) it is a trust and a choice for serving in the *construction of a community of faith* and for serving in the *apostolic mission of that community*.

---

11 In translating *pistós* by «trustworthy» (or credible) I am following A. Vanhoye's option, which seems to me the more probable one. Other authors say: «faithful and merciful». In any case, I think it is more important not to oppose both versions, since it is precisely the absolute *fidelity of Jesus to God* which makes him credible for us.

12 «We will be able to comfort those who are in any affliction with the comfort with which we ourselves are comforted by God» 2 Cor 1:4.

In relation to the first item (building up the community), the spirituality promoted must look for the greatest possible training and the minimum indispensable direction. The candidate should know, because of this, that the example and holiness demanded today of the ministry do not reside merely in the honesty of the personal life, but, above all, in the way of exercising the inevitable authority. Because there is only one way of exercising authority that is capable of really building community: that in which the authority is at the forefront when it is about exigencies and opening paths, but at the same time, fosters harmony and fraternity (even if it means remaining behind) where persons tend to impose themselves and prevail upon each other. The candidate must also know that the training for the ministry must not be seen as an «unavoidable bureaucratic requirement» to be forgotten after going through it, even less as an enrichment for personal advantage, but as a way of rapport —slow yet profound— between the Message and the person and —through the person— between the Message and the rest of humanity… and trying to be like Jesus in whom the Message and the Person correspond.

There is no need to stress that if what we said before questions many current ways of exercising authority in the Church, this questions many ways of studying (and teaching) theology today by those preparing for the ministry.

But we are talking not only of serving in the construction of the community, but also of serving the apostolic mission of said community, which is the main reason for its existence. We can dispense now with the *concrete form* of that apostolic mission, which should never proselytize or pursue anyone, but indeed should express at least the profound conviction that it is about the Good News and a «hidden treasure» to share. This simple detail is enough to understand that this second service will give the ecclesial ministry a spirituality of «constructor of history» to use a creative formula coined in the Conference of Puebla[13]. Constructor of history not to be lord of it but so the Church will never hear again the interpellation that even today the Father of Jesus seems to address to us: «Where were you when your Lord was being crucified?». So that the calvaries of this planet be not precisely the places where all the apostles and all the ecclesial ministries have disappeared and where there is only left a reduced remnant of faithful disciples, mostly women[14].

---

13 Puebla, n. 274: «school where people capable of making history be trained to effectively promote with Christ history… towards the Kingdom».

14 This is the oft-quoted statement of Jon Sobrino, with his peculiar sense of what is constitutive, it is not a clever «*boutade*» or a «cultivated pearl»: what the Church is most afraid of is not Marxism but God.

Well, I believe that in the New Testament there is a document which in a privileged way puts into action the exercise of a spirituality of this type. I am referring to the *Second Letter to the Corinthians* and all that Paul permits it to reveal about himself and his way of living the ministry. I will explain it briefly as a conclusion[15].

If we know how to distinguish between the proper *form* of the emotional temperament of Paul (probably debatable for some) and a Christological *content* expressed beneath that form, then I would say that this work of the New Testament should be the object of a slow and extended meditation in all so-called «Retreats for Orders»[16]. It is striking to ascertain how this letter has turned into *practical* attitudes what *Hebrews* presented as theological principles. Let us see this briefly.

a) The basis of everything

To begin with, the starting point is that, in Jesus Christ, *God has reconciled the world to Himself and gave us the ministry of that reconciliation* (cf. 5:18,19)[17]. We reached this same starting point in the analysis of *Hebrews* done in the first part. A starting point which —we said there— is not of worship but existential: Christological. The task of the ecclesial ministry is to build community: outwards (Kingdom of God) and inwards (people of God). From this it follows that the minister lives «constrained by that reconciling love of Christ» (5:14), and that the gift received by mercy (4:1) pushes the ministers unceasingly «not to live for themselves» (5:15) but «to comfort those who are in any affliction with the comfort with which we ourselves are comforted by God...» (1:4-6).

b) First consequence

—From this starting point emerges a first step in the forgetfulness of self: we do not proclaim ourselves but Christ Jesus (and ourselves as your servants for Jesus' sake: cf. 4:5).

—From this forgetfulness of self should follow identification with others which would lead them to proclaim: who is weak without my being weak? (11:29.30), and makes him even «rejoice when we ourselves are weak but you are strong» (13:9): since «my joy would be the joy of you all» (2:3) and «you are our

---

15 Here evidently we must forget all about exegetical discussions about the primitive text of the letter, or if our present text is a fusion of other letters. We will limit ourselves to take the text synchronically just as it has reached us.

16 And about the form, we should add that 2 Corinthians is a fraternal letter: from equal to equal, even when he is exercising his authority. Paul shows his weakness without clothing himself with sacredness. What bishop today could write such a direct letter to his diocese?

17 Or of a «new covenant» not of the letter but of the Spirit; it does not kill but gives life (3:6). These are parallel phrases.

letter of recommendation» (3:2), etc. This will mean for Paul not only extraordinary external difficulties (lashes, dangers, hunger…) but also the daily pressure of the «concern for all the churches» (11:24-28). This is why Paul even accepts «to be absent from the Lord» (5:6).

—Which means «not being *yes* and *no*, but a clear *yes*» to all the promises in each human being (cf. 1:19), since «I do not seek what is yours, but you» (12:14), and so we do not try to «lord it over your faith, but are workers with you for your joy» (1:24)[18].

c) Second consequence

And this generic attitude —similar to the «mercy» of the priest in *Hebrews*— is also, as it is there, the one that makes the minister «trustworthy»: «giving no cause for offense in anything, so that the ministry will not be discredited» (6:3) even if it means that we «spend and be expended for your souls» (12:15) or «in everything commending ourselves in afflictions, in hardships, in hunger…» (6:4). The signs of the Apostle are not miracles but «that I myself did not become a burden to you» (12:11-13).

d) An impossible program?

—It will not be easy. First, both the harshness of reality and the sin of humanity imply that, sometimes, the exercise of authority can «cause sadness». But Paul was very clear that if one must cause sadness, it should be sadness «according to the will of God» and not according to the world (7:10), because authority is *only* for building community and not for destroying it (10:8): we can do nothing *against* the truth but only for the truth (13:8). In this way of formulating this, Paul does not deviate an inch from the conditions the evangelist Matthew presented for the exercise of authority.

—Secondly, it will not be easy because of one's own sin. What Paul describes is the goal to achieve, but he also knows that the treasure is contained in earthen vessels (4:7) and he identifies perfectly the thorn in the flesh of one's own ego (12:8). About this God has told him clearly that he will never be free of it, so that he can only boast of his own weaknesses (11:30; 12:6,9) and that he can only count on the grace of God and not on himself for the exercise of his ministry… (12:9).

---

18 In the *First Letter to the Corinthians* he will add that because «I do all things for the sake of the gospel»… «I have become all things to all men (Greek, Jew, slave, weak…) so that I may by all means save some» (1Cor 9:18-22).

It is a splendid program and its credibility comes from its own attractiveness in spite of the fact that it is way above us. This panorama, although swift, is enough. If we ministers of the Church had not forgotten it perhaps it would not have been necessary to write today about the ecclesial ministry. But it must be so, because we all carry that treasure in earthen vessels...

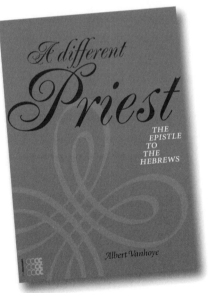

Rediscover the Historical Praxis of Jesus Through the Latest Research

A provocative and sensitive bestseller

This controversial book is now available in English for the first time. In this bestseller, greeted with both enthusiasm and controversy in Europe, Pagola, criticized by some of depicting a too-human Jesus, offers a scholarly and thought-provoking biblical rereading of the life of Jesus. Pagola reconstructs the complete historical figure of Jesus with a scholarly exegetical and theological approach, in an easy to read language.

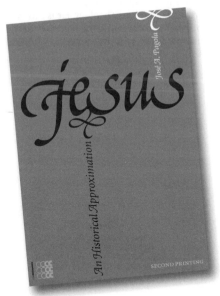

José Antonio Pagola was born in Spain in 1937. He completed his theological studies at the Pontifical Gregorian University and his studies in Sacred Scripture at the Pontifical Biblical Institute in Rome. He also studied Biblical sciences at the École Biblique in Jerusalem. He has dedicated his life to Biblical studies and Christology and has done research on the historical Jesus for more than 30 years, selling more than 60.000 copies of his recent theological Bestseller *Jesús. Aproximación histórica*, now available in English by Convivium Press.

A new perspective to study the Gospels of Mark, Matthew and Luke

Meynet offers an entirely new perspective on the study of the Synoptic Gospels, adding further insights within the growing body of modern research into the meanings of the Gospels of Maththew, Mark and Luke. Utilizing the rhetorical method of analysis, of wich he is leading proponent, Meynet studies the composition of the Gospels and makes it possible to understand them in systematic and until now unexpected ways.

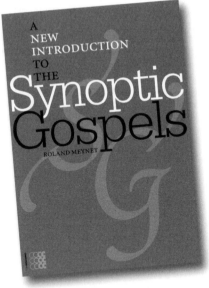

Roland Meynet S.J. is presently professor of Biblical theology at the Pontifical Gregorian University in Rome and was the former director of its Department of Biblical Theology. He is a founding member and currently the secretary of the International Society for the Studies of Biblical and Semitic Rhetoric.

Reclaiming the spirit and praxis of the reign of God

Post-resurrection communities continued to practice living in the reign of God. With the rise of Emperor Constantine, however, this vibrant counter-cultural movement of believers was institutionalized within the Roman Empire. Over time the institutional Church became the dominant power with all the trappings of empire. The author shows how this notion can change the face of Christianity.

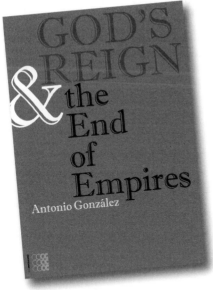

Is Life in Society Possible without Morality?

Sergio Bastianel answers the question by addressing the responsibility of Christians to confront issues of justice within society in ways that promote the common good. The author, who views one's relationship with the «other» as foundational to the moral experience, places a priority on human relationships based on sharing and solidarity. He emphasizes the interconnections between personal morals and social justice and raises fundamental questions about such issues as political life and economics, about hunger and development, and about the true meaning of «charity», all of which are relevant issues in our contemporary societies.

Sergio Bastianel s.j. is currently professor of moral theology at the Pontifical Gregorian University in Rome and also serves as its academic vice-rector. He spent his early years teaching and lecturing at the Pontifical Theological Faculty of San Luigi in Naples, Italy, and in later years he served as dean of the theological faculty of the Pontifical Gregorian University.

A beautiful and simple proposal to construct our Spiritual Life through Discernment and Prayer of the Heart

One of the greatest experts in the spirituality of Eastern Christianity, Cardinal Špidlík, deals in this book with prayer and spiritual life, with the experience of grace and goodness, through discernment of evil and human passions in everyday experience. It is a beautiful and simple proposal to construct our spiritual life through discernment and prayer of the heart.

Tomáš Špidlík was born in Boskovice, now in the Czech Republic, in 1919. In 1951, Špidlík began broadcasting programs from Vatican Radio calling for freedom behind the Iron Curtain. He met with Alexander Dubcek, former First Secretary of the Central Committee of the Communist Party of Czechoslovakia, and Václav Havel, who became President of Czechoslovakia. Špidlík is Professor of Eastern Spiritual Theology, and Cardinal, and is known as one of the greatest experts in Eastern Christianity today. He has been chosen «Man of the Year, 1990» and «the most admired person of the decade» by the American Bibliographical Institute of Raleigh in North Carolina.

Builders of Community:
Rethinking Ecclesiastical Ministry

This book was printed on *thin opaque smooth white Bible paper*, using the *Minion* and *Type Embellishments One* font families.
This edition was printed in D'VINNI, S.A., in Bogotá, Colombia, during the last weeks of the sixth month of year two thousand twelve.

Ad publicam lucem datus mense junii Sacri Cordis Iesus